D1242601

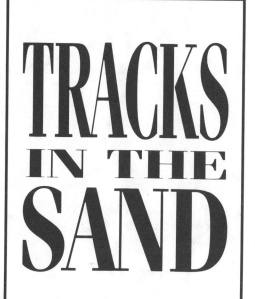

TRACKS IN THE SAND

Your Guide
To Recovery
Journaling

Dr. Vance L. Shepperson
Dr. Bethyl Joy Shepperson

Thomas Nelson Publishers
Nashville

This book is dedicated to the parents who died while
it was being birthed:
Rev. Edward Midura
and
Mrs. Flournoy Shepperson, Jr.

Library of Congress Cataloging-in-Publication Data

Shepperson, Vance L.
    Tracks in the sand : your guide to recovery journaling /
Vance L. Shepperson, Bethyl Joy Shepperson.
        p.   cm.
    Includes bibliographical references.
    ISBN 0-8407-3376-3 (pbk.)
    1. Self-actualization (Psychology)—Problems, exercises, etc.
2. Diaries—Therapeutic use. 3. Diaries—Authorship. 4. Self
-actualization (Psychology)—Religious aspects—Christianity.
5. Diaries—Authorship—Religious aspects—Christianity.
I. Shepperson, Bethyl Joy. II. Title. III. Title: Recovery
journaling.
BF637.S4S51774   1992
158'.1—dc20   92–20141
                                                        CIP

Printed in the United States of America
1 2 3 4 5 6 7 — 97 96 95 94 93 92

CONTENTS

Chapter 1   Butterflies Come from Cocoons   *1*

Chapter 2   Journaling to Recover from Addiction   *23*

Chapter 3   Recovering from Depression Through Journaling   *42*

Chapter 4   The Dream Journal   *61*

Chapter 5   Journaling for Men   *76*

Chapter 6   Journaling for Women   *93*

Chapter 7   The Couple's Journal   *106*

Chapter 8   Journaling About Your Family of Origin   *126*

Notes   *150*

Bibliography   *152*

About the Authors   *154*

# ACKNOWLEDGMENTS

The labor pains that birthed this book were sharp ones. During this period of our lives we experienced some crisis and much change. Vance's mother committed suicide; Bethyl's dad died of a heart attack; Vance went through his own version of a mid-life crisis; and our counseling practice survived a harrowing recession. Throughout this time our friends and family supported and encouraged us. We've recovered from our own dysfunctions and addictions with their support, love, and confrontations.

We thank especially Tony and Marion Fortosis, Earl Henslin, Karen Pierpoint, Steve and Patti Cappa, Sam and Judy Doolittle, and Jackie Shumway. They're good, salt-of-the-earth people; we need and enjoy them as friends.

We salute Bethyl's mom, Alice Midura, for enduring the loss of her husband of fifty-two years and for birthing a renewed, lively relationship with us.

We appreciate our editors, Ron Haynes, Jane Jones, and Harriet Crosby. Their patient guidance and support have made the labor pains pay off with a live birth and healthy child!

We appreciate each other. As husband and wife we've found new joy and respect for each other during this labor of love, and we thank God each day for blessing our marriage.

Most of all we give our love to our Heavenly Parent, who does all things well, grounds us, and gives us hope in our recovery journeys.

FOREWORD

The Christian community has experienced important changes in the past ten years. The Holy Spirit has moved in the church, and Christians are having a time of revival—a time to heal the inner hurts that hinder their relationships with God, with themselves, and with others. Men, women, and children now feel an increasing freedom to discuss honestly and openly their recoveries from alcoholism, drug addiction, sexual addiction, codependency, homosexuality, and physical, emotional, and sexual abuses. This recovery movement has encouraged the formation of support and Twelve-Step groups in churches throughout the United States and around the world. In addition, the Christian community has responded to the recovery movement with the publication of a number of Bible-based books that deal more sincerely and directly with addictions and abuses than those of previous decades. This very special time in the history of the church is laying the foundation for the Christian community to truly become a healing community.

As this recovery movement grows, there is an aching cry for the practical tools that can help us deal with the deep wounds we carry from the past, as well as the struggles we each face in the present. Too many writers describe the problem, yet do not give realistic suggestions for steps to take in the recovery process. Drs. Vance and Bethyl Shepperson do provide practical tools in this book, *Tracks in the Sand: Your Guide to Recovery Journaling.*

Many times in my work I have asked clients to journal about specific issues, yet have been unable to show them how to turn their writing experiences into events rich in newfound truth and inner awareness. *Tracks in the Sand* gives the guidelines I've been missing. Put into practice these tips will deepen anyone's recovery journey. Like the difference between reading a book about the Grand Canyon and visiting the park itself, *Tracks in the Sand* moves you beyond merely keeping a journal to a thoughtful sorting out of who you are. It leaves you a changed person, ready to take new steps and risks.

Many who write recovery books share their knowledge about recovery, but reveal little of themselves. As you read and use the tools and suggestions in this book you will find yourself participating in the struggles, the pain, and the personal journeys of the authors. They share candidly and frankly about their pain and the dark times they have been through. This book was not written from a distance, but from the intimate struggles of two people who love the Lord and love each other and who seek to grow and change. The Sheppersons strive to confront the past so that it does not tear them from each other and from God.

Vance and Bethyl have been my close friends for the past ten years. They have given me support, and I admire and respect them for making it through the hurt and pain in their lives. This book is a sharing of themselves—the selves that have cried, the selves that have felt the anger and the pain, and the selves that have found the little boy or girl within who is ready to play and to be close. Their work as psychologists in Southern California is highly respected, and they are sought out by many who are struggling with those deep and painful times in life. This book is a must for anyone beginning or already in recovery.

Earl R. Henslin

1

Butterflies

Come

from

Cocoons

Why Journal?

Solitude is the mother country of the great, for it is often in solitude that we recover from life's wounds. We have the chance to be quiet, feel our feelings, grow, and change. Over the last two decades our journals have allowed us this purposive solitude.

They've been our twenty-four hour a day, seven day a week individual recovery sponsors—always available, always comforting. They've helped us grow up emotionally. And they've also been our private marital counselor, allowing us increased closeness as a couple.

Our journal records of our thoughts, struggles, victories, and debacles have given them substance, for without this solitary time, we would have sometimes wondered if our inner worlds were real. Journaling has allowed us a unique way to probe our wounds and wonderments. We've been in touch with our dreams, strengths, and successes. We've also learned more of how to recover from our nightmares, weaknesses, and past failures.

Journaling is like rubbing your finger across the grain of your soul. Sometimes your finger feels smoothness and sometimes you pick up a splinter. But always it is an aid to a personal journey of hope. For us, our journals have often been the only places available where we could discover who we've been, who we are now, and who we are becoming. They have provided us with the unique opportunity to effect change from the inside out. They've been records of the desert through which we've wandered; they have been our tracks in the sand.

From the Inside Out

Most people recovering from various forms of abuse and dysfunction are chronically hungry and thirsty for emotional and spiritual nourishment. But most of us recovery journeyers, including Bethyl and me, long for others to feed us. We look to our parents, our family and friends, our marriage partners, our pastors to feed us. And we take in this nourishment, trying to use it to grow and feel better. But as important as this food might be, it doesn't change us. We don't change because of outside influences. We change because of inside influences. Transforming growth in life takes place first on the inside and then works its way out into our actions and attitudes. This type of from-the-inside-out growth needs comfort, stillness, and containment to take place.

Our journals have been like cocoons where this growth can occur. We have become in-formed about our recovery. We've taken shape and been transformed in our journaling cocoons. Old, used up ways of crawling through life have died there and new ways of recovering have been born and given wings.

The insights we gain in the journaling cocoon are like little flashlights that help us see ahead into the dark places of recovery. This intuitive seeing, this in-sight, allows sufficient light for us to see the butterflies we are becoming. And when we're falling apart, as we all do in our recoveries, our journals become safe places to observe that process.

We know that changing is very hard work. None of us can recover from life's wounds without support, guidance, and the right tools. Our journals have been our friends, counselors, and sponsors. Your journal can be these to you as well. Journaling helps recovery; it points you in the direction of becoming more free.

The purpose of this interactive workbook is to teach you, step by step, to more effectively in-form yourself as you find in-sight in your recovery process. We offer detailed guidelines to help you leave behind your old addictions and dysfunctions. These guidelines encourage you to become free through journaling. During this time we'll have some fun playing, learning new skills, and in-forming different, more grown-up selves. We'll help a butterfly emerge from your cocoon.

Connecting With God

When you journal, not only do you get to know yourself, you also move beyond yourself to God. The boundaries of your soul get penciled in. They become visible to you as you begin to hear God's voice.

A client once asked, "How can I get God's voice louder?" and I replied, "His voice is as loud as it's going to get. Some other places in the rest of your life have to become more quiet."

For those of us who choose to journal, the journaling cocoon is a place where the noise of our lives can wear itself out. When we get used to the quiet, we can hear God speaking to us and begin to recover spiritually.

We need spiritual recovery, just as we need relationship recovery, if we are to be whole again. We need to hear God's voice. We need to slip into our cocoons and learn to listen.

While you are learning to hear God speak to you, you could think about the many ways we know him and the names we use to refer to him. Not only is he the Father, Son, and Holy Spirit, he is also the Rock of Ages, the Shepherd, the Lamb, a mother hen, an eagle. For many in recovery it is helpful, even essential, to embrace the many images of God, for one or more of his images could bring to mind a painful, wounding experience. For example, the parent image of God the Father could relate in your mind to painful experiences with your human father, and temporarily cause you great discomfort. However, relating to God with his alternative images could be redemptive.

The Family of Self

When I was a small boy, my father told me this little rhyme:

> Three in one,
> One in three,
> And the one in the middle
> died for me.

By teaching me this rhyme, my dad was trying to help me understand the concept of one God who is Father, Son, and Holy Spirit. As a child I understood that a father (my dad) was one person and a son (me) was a separate person. It was a while before I could understand that one person could be all three. My dad, for example, was my father, his father's son, and his friend's friend. Then I could grasp that, just as the one Creator God is Father, Son, and Holy Spirit, we are all also both one and many—we are each one person with many part-selves. And all our part-selves are members of our own inner households, even those we've forgotten.

When Bethyl was a small girl, for example, she was throwing a pillow in her aunt's living room and accidentally broke some glass figurines. She was humiliated. Because she was so shamed, she learned to forget the part of her that enjoyed roughhousing and being playful. What she forgot, she lost.

Losing part-selves follows a pattern. First we forget; then we forget we forgot. The landscapes of our souls are gradually covered and then lost under this gentle, gradual snowfall of amnesia. If we want to recover wholeness in our lives, we must remember and make friends with all our part-selves, especially those we've lost along the way.

Journaling helps you re-member yourself. You re-member when you join together again the members of your self who've been lost. Only as you are re-membered do you have a chance to recover.

We're each a full family of different part-selves, many of whom have been forgotten. Within us we have conservatives rubbing elbows with communists, Judases with saints, and murderers with martyrs. If I want to recover some sense of wholeness in my life, I need to re-member and make friends with the members of my own household. The parts of me that I've forgotten I will often see in others, for the intense feelings we have toward others often belong to the parts of ourselves we've forgotten.

To use my dad as an example again, one of his selves is his father-self. He had certain feelings, reactions, beliefs, and so forth when I was a young boy. He had different ones when I was a teen and still different ones when I was an adult. His father-self changed over time, but the make-up of his father-selves at each stage are still within him, even if he has consciously forgotten them.

In the same way, his son- and friend-selves throughout his life are still parts of who he was and who he became. Dad forgot some of these selves along the way. Meeting them again, making friends with them (perhaps for the first time), would give him a new perspective on who he is and who he will become. It is the same for Bethyl in her work of making friends again with her roughhousing, playing child-selves.

This re-membering helps heal the wounds and redefine the boundaries of the soul. It allows change from the inside out and makes recovery possible. This poem illustrates one person's understanding of his experience in meeting and learning about his part-selves.

Do not say that I'll depart tomorrow
Because even today I still arrive.

Look at me: I arrive in every second
To be a bud on a spring branch,
To be a tiny bird in my new nest,
To be a caterpillar in the heart of a flower,
To be a jewel hiding itself in a stone.

The rhythm of my heart is the birth and death
Of all that are alive. . . .

I am a frog swimming happily
In the clear water of a pond,
And I am also the grass snake who,
Approaching in silence, feeds itself on the frog.

I am the twelve-year-old girl, a refugee on a small boat,
Who throws herself into the ocean
After being raped by a sea pirate.
I am also the pirate,
My heart not yet capable of seeing and loving. . . .

Please call me by my true names
So that I can hear all my cries and my laughs at once,
So I can see that my joy and my pain are one. . . .

Please call me by my true names
So I can wake up. . . .[1]

—Thich Nhat Hanh

In and Then Out

Do you ever feel like a car that is up to its hubcaps in the sand? That is when you feel like you are spinning your wheels, going nowhere, but getting deeper and deeper in your problems. Journaling is a way of digging out. But just as you must use a rocking motion to actually get your car out of the sand, being careful not to go in one direction for too long, you must temper your inner work with moving out to be with others.

If you spend too much time alone, you lose your contact with others and become isolated. If you spend too much time with someone else, you lose your sense of your self and become co-dependent.

Journaling is a way of being only with your self. Used creatively, it also offers you a meaningful way of being with others. You can go in for a while and attend to your inner work. Then you can come out, using what you've learned about your self, relating to others in more satisfying ways. In, then out. In and out. This is the rocking motion that will get you out of the sand of addiction and dysfunction.

Journaling Exercises

As you use this book, you will read a little and then write a little. The exercises will gradually introduce you to the journaling experience. We already know that the most difficult part of journaling is getting started. This is what Roseanne Lloyd and Richard Solly, in their book *Journey Notes,* call the problem of "showing up at the ball park." This little problem isn't something you will meet and conquer just once or twice. It will come back again and again.

We have both encountered problems with "showing up at the ball park." Sometimes I live my life driven by the tyranny of the urgent. I move quickly through the day, stomping out brush fires, until I collapse with exhaustion. Because journaling is an activity I consider important, but not urgent, I tend to journal only when I'm not frantically running from crisis to stupor. Bethyl's tendency is to be more faithful than I am, but she also is sometimes too busy to journal.

This first exercise will help you make an honest appraisal of how you live your life. It will help you assess the amount of time you stake out for living as opposed to whether you merely allow life to run you through the wringer while you're not looking. This is a warm-up exercise. After all, you're at the ball park right now; you might as well warm up and see how journaling works.

Exercise	Review your activity calendar for the past week and then write a letter to yourself detailing how much time you saved during the week for important but not urgent matters. Compare these times to other times when you were tyrannized by life's urgencies. Be sure to date and sign your letter.

Selecting Your Tools

This book teaches several ways to journal. We will discuss journaling for daily living, for healing different wounded areas of life (such as depression or addictive behavior), for men, for women, and for recording and understanding dreams. We will also teach couples how to journal together, and we will help you mine treasures from the family in which you grew up. Before you begin, however, you will want to select your tools.

Journals take many forms and you can choose to use the tools that you most enjoy. Journaling should be a pleasure, so make the most of it.

What Kind of Journal Is Right for You?

I prefer using a word processor because my fingers can fly over the keyboard, keeping up with my thoughts. Bethyl writes in long hand using hardback books. A friend has a more traditional journal with a lock and key. Another friend uses a three-ring binder that she keeps in a safe place, adding pages as they come "hot off the press." Others write their thoughts on scraps of paper that they throw in a drawer.

Deciding the way you will journal may seem relatively unimportant, but for many the type of journal they use makes a difference. You should decide what form of journaling will be right for you.

What Writing Instrument Will You Use?

Next you'll need to decide the kind of tool to use for writing. Some people need a special pen or pencil. Others use a typewriter or a computer. You might want to use pens of different colors for different occasions or to differentiate needs, emotions, or parts of the self. Perhaps you would enjoy using a fine point pen suitable for calligraphy.

As you change, the kind of journal and the writing instruments that bring you pleasure will also change. Be curious. Experiment and see what you can find that best fits you now.

Pick Your Place and Time

Picking the place where you will journal and the time when you will journal are just as important as deciding how you will write and what you will write in. Perhaps deciding the time and place are the most important decisions you will make, for they are connected with showing up at the ball park.

You will want to make an appointment with yourself. Put you on your calendar. It will help you avoid the crisis-to-stupor problem I sometimes have and the "I'm tired today; I'll do it tomorrow" problems others have.

The place where you will journal is important, too. You might choose a particular chair in your bedroom or perhaps the right place is the kitchen table early in the morning before anyone else is up. The place you choose needs to be private, and you should be able to establish some boundaries concerning how and when you will be disturbed by others during this time.

Journaling Techniques

Now that you have chosen a journal, a writing instrument, and a private place for journaling, it is time to actually begin writing. Sometimes a blank page in a journal can be intimidating and you can't think of a thing to write about. Before you have even begun, you suffer from that dreaded disease—writer's block!

When this happens, try a few of the following techniques. Some of them are borrowed from Lloyd and Solly. These techniques are also designed to be fun. Practice each one with a sense of playfulness. Journaling is an enjoyable experience.

Detail Your Day

Your journal is a place to capture and experience your emotional life, for exploring your emotions is crucial to your recovery. The more you are able to capture the details of the day in your journal, the more you will be able to explore the emotions that are a part of your daily experience. When recording your day, remember to record as many details and facts as possible. Details offer important clues about our emotional lives and the choices we make during each day. For example, compare the following two journal accounts of the same event:

Today I spoke with Bob. I worried the nail on my ring finger, chewing it in quick stolen snatches whenever he looked down at his lap. I rocked back and forth in my oversized judge's chair, my breathing went shallow, and my gaze fixed somewhere in the middle of his forehead. After eleven minutes of this, Bob casually mentioned that he had just been fired.

Today I got anxious when Bob told me he'd been fired.

When you choose an event from your day and write down every fact, detail, and thought about it, you gain important information about how you connect emotionally with the world. Focus on how your body responded to an event. This helps your emotional world become three dimensional, rich, and exciting. When you write this way, writer's block is past history!

Write the Way You Talk

Often we suffer writer's block when we feel a subtle pressure to write perfect prose. But a journal is not a place for great literature. It is a place where you can pour out your heart. When writing in your journal, it is best to speak your mind and heart simply, honestly, and directly, as if you are talking to your best friend. Blocks to journaling happen only when you think: How would so-and-so say this? Am I writing correctly? Would I be embarrassed if someone read this? It doesn't matter! Your journal is just for you, so remember to write in it the way you speak in ordinary conversation. In other words, write the way you talk.

Write Automatically

The best way to write like you talk is to write automatically. Forget grammar, punctuation, and spelling. Just let the words flow automatically from your fingertips onto the page of your journal.

Some folks like to watch their hand move across the page as though they are looking over someone else's shoulder, watching this other person write. You may want to experiment with this technique.

Exercise

Give yourself some relaxation suggestions before you try automatic writing. Take some deep, easy breaths. Everything is getting comfortably heavy; your arms and legs are comfortably heavy; your thoughts and feelings are floating by like a lazy river.

Next, say to your hand, "I'll just be relaxed and curious about what you, a hand with a pen in it, want to write in my journal. OK, hand, do your stuff! Just begin. Draw, scribble, write like a baby, or do whatever you want. I'm not responsible for you. Go for it!" Finally, let your hand write freely across the page. Adopt a curious, compassionate attitude. See what happens.

Confront the Critic

When you are practicing automatic writing or other journaling exercises, your inner critic sometimes might pop up. We all have one who occasionally criticizes our journal writing. When your critic tries to stop you from writing, try this technique.

Exercise

Talk to your inner critic. Imagine your critic is a real person and have a conversation with him or her. Then record the conversation in your journal. First, write whatever you want to say to your critic. Make sure you give your critic a piece of your mind! Then change places with him or her, imagining that you are your critic. Answer back by writing a response to yourself in your journal. Again, don't pull any punches—be as nasty a critic as you want.

While writing this book, I had a writer's block and I tried this technique to get beyond it. This is an excerpt from my journal:

My critic is dressed in a long, black robe. His black hair is slicked down. His face is pinched, his nose is aquiline, his eyes are sunken. He has no love for me.

what are you doing here: *why are you trying to stop me?*	*WHAT AM I DOING HERE?* *YOU'LL NEVER BE ABLE TO* *WRITE A BOOK!*
what is it to you if i succeed? *it seems like you are only* *interested in keeping me down.*	*I AM FROM YOUR FATHER'S* *PAST AND HIS FATHER BEFORE* *HIM. WE ALL LIVED IN OUR* *HEADS AND NOT IN OUR* *HEARTS. NOW WE STAND* *GUARD TO KEEP YOU OUT OF* *YOUR HEART. WE WON'T LET A* *TRAITOR IN THE HOUSE.*
i can write this book and not be a *traitor. let's make a deal—you are* *good with words and i'm good* *with feelings. alone, neither of us* *will succeed—but together we can* *write this book.*	*WELL, I'LL GIVE IT A SHOT.*

When you confront your critic and allow your critic to speak, you put to rest for a time your critic's fears, and your own fears, about writing your feelings.

Write in a Rush

Rush writing is similar to automatic writing. In automatic writing, words flow out of your pen at their own pace. Writing in a rush, however, means letting all of your thoughts and feelings come out on paper quickly. Again, don't let grammar, punctuation, or spelling censor what you write. Don't try to edit rush writing, but let pearls of wisdom rest side by side with emotional trash.

Rush writing often helps you get past writing blocks that come from an overly critical, conscious mind. It encourages the appearance of your unconscious self on paper. You will be surprised how much inner wisdom your unconscious self wants to share with you. It's a lot smarter than you think.

Drawing and Art Work

Some people have trouble exploring their inner, emotional worlds using only words. Instead, they prefer to use images. Sometimes feelings won't be bottled onto a printed line. During such times, you may want to experiment with drawing in your journal, or creating a work of art outside of your journal and writing about it later.

Lucia Capacchione, in *The Creative Journal*, focuses on journaling as the "art of finding yourself." This little volume is written from an art therapist's point of view. It is invaluable in exploring the self that lies beyond words. This is particularly useful for those young members of the family of self who haven't learned very many words to express themselves.

When experimenting with drawing or art as a journaling technique, be sure to work with materials that make the experience fun. Experiment and play with finger-painting, sketching with pencil, making collages, scribbling, or even modeling clay. Let your imagination run wild. All of these are possible tools for making tracks in the sand.

Using art and drawing is another, different kind of journaling. But once you have finished drawing or creating a piece of art, try to record in your journal your feelings about the experience.

Dance and Movement

Occasionally even art or drawing are not helpful ways of expressing our deepest feelings. When words and art just aren't enough, try putting on some music that fits your feeling and moving with it. Flow with the serene; jive with the exciting; pound with the angry; waltz with the romantic.

After moving or dancing to the music of your mood, try recording your experience in your journal. Pay particular attention to the dancing interplay between feelings and movement, your emotional life and how your body expresses emotion. In other words, let your body do the talking through your journal pages!

If you are feeling brave enough, you may want to try recording your dance or movement on videotape and, later, watch yourself move to your emotional mood. In other words, the videotape becomes your journal. Watching your dance on video may help you gain new insight and perspective into your emotional patterns. Be aware, though, of your inner critic as you experiment with video journaling. Cultivate compassion toward your critic as well as your video journaling efforts.

Take Short Breaks

When journaling, give yourself permission to take short breaks. Sometimes you may come up against a writer's block simply because you need a break. When that happens, get up and stretch. Take a walk. Pray. Do something different and let whatever is in your cocoon incubate awhile more. Let whatever is growing within you have time to grow. The journal will be there when you return.

Problems with Journaling

The Dark Side of Journaling

Sometimes journaling is a way of staying too long in the dark. It can be like a day-long sour lollipop or a way of going into the backyard to eat worms. Life isn't going well and we're going to luxuriate in this misery—page after page after numbing page. Beware of letting your journal turn into one endless tale of woe. Using your journal only to record unhappy events and feelings may result in your giving up on the process of writing altogether. So make sure you journal the good times, as well as the bad.

Another danger is that you might use your journal to avoid people. If people scare you and you avoid dealing with relationship problems, your journal can be a stagnant haven. Used well, journaling will improve your outer relationships.

It is possible to minimize these potential dangers of journaling by integrating your inner emotional world with your outer action world. Insight needs to be married to emotion and action if substantial change is to take place. The insight you gain from journaling gives light for effective action. But action must follow or the insight is worse than useless.

However, for most journalers, acting on insight isn't the problem. Journaling is a strenuous challenge for those who are impulse and action oriented. For those who are "working the program" without feeling or thought, journaling will instruct, guide, and slow them down. For these action oriented folks, journaling is not something they have tried and found difficult, it is something they have found difficult and have not tried.

We Before Me

Dysfunctional people from dysfunctional families are mostly selfless; they have little or no self. For these people, the hard work of character formation, of time spent in the cocoon, was by-passed at a very early age. They were taught to be part of a *we*, before they learned to be a *me*. In other words, people from dysfunctional families have no identities, no sense of self apart from their diseased family relationships.

Carl Jung, the famous psychoanalyst, once said that we often spend the first half of our lives living out our parents' unlived lives. Then after becoming miserable enough, we decide to recover ourselves and live our own lives. Journaling is a wake-up call that will allow us to live our own lives instead of someone else's. Your journal helps you find your healthy self, who in-forms you and enriches all your external relationships.

I Don't Have Anything to Say

When beginning a journal, you may view your life as an endless stream of drivel punctuated by little blips of something noteworthy. You believe you just don't have anything to say.

As an example of this kind of thinking, one of my clients told me, "If I write down who I am, I'm afraid it will be a very short story!" The only way to deal with such fear is to make direct contact with it. Another man once told me that the few times he spent journaling, the experience was like entering at the middle of a foreign movie without subtitles. He was puzzled by his inner world, and he was tempted to give up writing about it. Instead, he opened his journal and simply began writing about his fear and the block he was experiencing. He began to understand his inner world only after he faced his fear of not understanding or having enough to write about. When you are feeling this way, first remember that your journal will help you recover your best, healthy self. You have plenty to write about.

Dreams offer a great deal of material to write about in your journal. But dreams often seem nonsensical instead of important clues to recovering your healthy, best self. In his book *Inner Work*, Robert Johnson tells the story of a man who dreamed he was in a ravine, cutting his way with a machete through a thick jungle. The going was tough. When, after a long while, he reached the roaring river at the base of the gorge, he found someone cutting an identical path to the river from the other side of the gorge. The lesson of this dream is that when we seek our unconscious selves, our unconscious selves seek us. If you use your journal to search for clues for your best, healthy self, your unconscious self will meet you and be your guide to recovery.

Active Imagination

Everybody loves a good story. Using the process of active imagination will help you tell a good story—your own personal story of recovering your self. Active imagination is a technique that uses inner images and dialogues with those images to discover the story your inner, mainly unconscious self wants to tell you during your recovery. Active imagination is a learned skill. It doesn't happen automatically. It takes a little practice to tell a story well. The art of telling stories is the hallmark of effective teachers, preachers, and public speakers.

The greatest teacher of all time was Jesus. The Bible says he only spoke to the people in parables, and "without a parable He did not speak to them."[2] He told healing stories that fit the people of his day. Active imagination is a technique that will allow you to create your own healing parables in the service of your own healing.

Robert Johnson's book, *Inner Work*, details four practical steps for using active imagination as part of the journaling process. The first step is to create a living room in your soul where you can invite all the various family members who live inside you. This creates a willing emotional space where you can learn more about the different parts of your self. In your inner living room, you must always be willing to see, listen to, and welcome all the images and voices of your deepest self.

For example, recently I had a dream where I found myself frantically trying to take care of a large family that had moved in with me. I heard a knock on the door. When I answered, a little blond girl, about three years old, was standing there. She said, "You went off and left me. Isn't this my house too?" I recognized her as my own little girl, and with great compassion I picked her up and welcomed her home.

The second step in using active imagination involves dialogue between you and your inner images. Entering into dialogue with the many parts of your self requires courage.

You must clearly imagine each part of your self and listen very carefully to each image. Asking the following questions will help you get a clear picture of each image or part of your self. Who is talking to you? Does this image have a name? What does he or she look like? How is the image dressed? Are you meeting him or her in a house, in a room, outdoors? Describe your surroundings. What kind of posture, tone of voice, or attitude does the image have toward you? Is the image hostile, loving, kind, wise, upset? Once you have a clear picture in your imagination of this part of your self, you are ready to listen and respond to the image in your journal.

When I dialogue with other parts of my self, I use lowercase letters for one part of me and all capitals for the other part. I use no punctuation when writing the dialogue in my journal because punctuation would only slow me down. Another useful dialoging tactic is to arrange your dialogue by assigning one part of your self to the left side of the page and another part to the right side of the page. Draw a line down the middle of the page to separate the two part-selves.

As an example, let's use my dream about the little blond girl coming home. My dialogue with her would look like this:

I'M SO SORRY I FORGOT ABOUT YOU	yes you do that a lot i have to keep coming back and reminding you that i'm around
THANKS FOR BEING BETTER ABOUT THAT THAN I AM I'LL TRY HARDER TO LOVE YOU BETTER	ok

Another technique for recording active imagination dialogue is to use your dominant hand when writing the voice of your most conscious self. Then change hands and use your non-dominant hand to record the voice of the part of your self that comes up from your unconscious. As you move back and forth in the dialogue between these two voices, you will find changing writing hands will help bring new awareness to these different parts of you.

Now let's put imagination and dialogue all together to give expression to your many inner selves. Remember to focus on the sight, sound, and feel of your part-self once it appears in your inner living room. After carefully listening to this part-self speak, communicate to your part-self or image what you saw and heard. It is crucial that your inner image feel it is being taken seriously and that your conscious self is hearing its voice.

Going back to my example of my little girl coming home, I might say to her:

I KNOW YOU FEEL
ABANDONED BY ME. THAT
MUST BE CONFUSING AND
HURT A LOT.

Then let your inner image or part-self know what you, your conscious self, think and feel in this experience. Continuing with the little girl example:

I FEEL REALLY BAD THAT I DO
THIS TO YOU OVER AND OVER
AGAIN.

Listen again to what your image may have to say in response. My little girl might have responded:

you keep saying that and then
leaving me out in the cold—i'm
not sure i believe you.

17

Go back and forth in this dialoging until you and your part-self have nothing further to say to each other at present.

The third step in using active imagination is attaching value to the image of your part-self and what has been said in the dialogue. Read over the dialogue recorded in your journal and see if it fits with your sense of right and wrong. If an inner image is being hurtful or unfair, then you may want to have another dialogue exploring the hurt or lack of fairness. Healing is only possible once we discover the source of a wound or wrong. Attaching value to a dialogue and exploring it further is an excellent way to get at the source of pain and let healing begin.

The last step to using active imagination is creating a ritual that honors the image and dialogue recorded in your journal. In this step, you give the inner work outer expression. You take what you wrote in your journal and put it to work in your life. In my case, I needed to find a meaningful way to re-direct my care giving skills to the little blond girl, my inner child. The ritual I created was to set aside a regular time to play and rest. I refused to take on a new client at the counseling center. Creating a regular playtime was how I honored my dream and used valuable information given to me by my inner child.

Re-read your dialogue with your part-self. Ask yourself "What is this image trying to teach me about my self? Is there a way I can make an external change in my life to reflect this teaching?" If so, create a ritual or practice in your journal that shows how you are going to implement change in your external world.

Exercise

Practice an active imagination exercise designed to introduce you to the various rooms and chambers as different parts of your self. You will use your imagination first. After completing the imagination part of the exercise, you will record your experience in your journal.

You may practice the active imagination part of this exercise in three ways. Read the exercise until you see a series of dots (. . .) then close your eyes and imagine the scene being described. When you've finished imagining the scene, continue reading until you reach the next series of dots, and so on. You may want to have someone read the exercise to you, while you listen with your eyes closed. Or you may read the exercise into a tape recorder, pausing a while each time you encounter a series of dots. Only after completing the active imagination part of the exercise do you write of your experience in your journal.

Now you are ready to begin.

Rooms and Chambers   You are blindfolded and sitting in a small, dark room. As the door opens you hear a strong, but gentle voice greet you by name. That voice is your guide. Hear your name being called. . . .

The guide asks you to come along. Put your hand on the guide's shoulder. . . . The guide opens a door and leads you into a hallway. Smell the mustiness of the hallway. Listen as your heels click on the stone floor. You and your guide begin descending a circular staircase. You lose track of how far down you've gone. Feel yourself descending the stairs with your guide. . . .

Now you arrive at a level place. Your guide tells you that your blindfold is about to be removed and that you are in front of a full-length mirror. Your guide tells you that the person you are about to see in the mirror is a part of you who is a stranger. Your blindfold is removed and you stare at your own image in the mirror. . . .

Who is it you see? Notice how your image in the mirror is dressed. Observe the age of your image. What is your image's role and position in life? Observe as many details as possible in your image. . . .

Now look at your guide. Is your guide male or female? Young or old? How is your guide dressed? Observe as many details as possible about your guide. . . .

Become aware of your body. Notice your breathing—if you are taking short, shallow breaths, slow down and take long, deep breaths. . . .

Your guide now leads you down a long corridor. Many doors open off this corridor which stretches out into blackness. Each of the countless doors is shaped differently. Each door has a name engraved on a plaque beside it. You look at the names of the doors as you walk past. A few of the names you read are Pleasure, Faith, Anger, Sadness, Joy, and Loneliness. Finally, your guide stops at the room you are to enter. Read the name beside this door. . . .

Notice the door before you and how you are to enter the room. Do you need a key? If so, your guide supplies one. Does the door have a doorknob or is it a swinging door? Is the door made of glass or wood? Does the door have iron bars or is it shrouded with curtains?. . . .

You enter the room with your guide. Use your senses to observe the room. You hear. . . . You smell. . . . You see. . . . You feel. . . .

Move around the room and explore it in detail. . . . Observe how the room is furnished. Was someone inside waiting for you when you and your guide arrived? If so, allow conversation to develop, find out whether this room is his or her home, and discover why he or she lives in this particular room. . . .

When you have thoroughly explored this room and its occupant, say good-bye to it and leave with your guide. Your guide leads you back along the corridor, up the stairs, and returns you to the small, dark room where you began your journey.

Let this scene fade slowly from your imagination.

Now open your journal and record your journey. Write about your feelings and encounters as you discovered the many rooms that make up your self. Detail your experience of the room your guide selected for you to explore. Feel free to return to this exercise to explore a different room, a different part of your self.

How to Use This Book

All the chapters that follow may not be of immediate interest to everyone. Each one explores a different kind of journaling for specific needs and goals. For example, women may want to read the chapter, "Journaling for Men," after completing the chapter, "Journaling for Women." Not everyone who reads this book is part of a couple. If you are not a part of a couple, you may want to skip the chapter on "The Couple's Journal." From this point on, you choose which chapter you would like to read next. Feel free to work in each chapter as long as you like.

Repeat the exercises, re-read sections, and work in the chapter until you feel ready to move on to another one.

Before beginning a new chapter, ask God to bless your journal. Ask God to speak to you through your journal. Expect God to reach you and heal you as you write in your journal.

Approach each chapter with a sense of play. Journaling is an enjoyable activity, a time for being creative. Allow yourself to be curious about what flows from you onto the page.

You do not have to write in your journal all the time. Keep your journal and this workbook on a shelf until you feel an urge to play or go deeper into your inner world.

Should you encounter an exercise that does not feel right for you, don't do it. It could be the time isn't right for you to practice that particular exercise. Simply skip it and come back to it later. You will know when it is right to write.

Finally, it is always helpful to consciously relax. You will be most creative and imaginative when relaxed and living comfortably in your body. Use the following relaxation exercise before attempting exercises that use your imagination.

Exercise

You may want to tape record this exercise, reading it in a quiet voice. Or you may want to have a friend read it to you. Or you may simply read it and follow the instructions as you go. Remember to pause at each series of dots (. . . .).

First, find a quiet place where you can be alone for about fifteen minutes. If possible, lie down and stretch out flat on your back. If it isn't impossible to find a place to lie down, sit comfortably in a chair with your feet flat on the floor, your back straight, and your hands resting on top of your thighs.

Now close your eyes and breathe deeply a few times. . . . Feel your muscles begin to relax and grow heavy with each breath. . . . Start at the top of your head and feel your muscles relax throughout your body, all the way to the bottoms of your feet. . . . Let your whole body surrender to gravity. Each muscle in your body experiences nothing but quiet, calm, and comfort. . . . Let go of the cares of the day. There is nothing to do now. Let go and allow your mind to unwind. . . . Picture all the day's events like scribble covering a green chalkboard in front of you. Slowly, a hand begins to erase all the scribble until nothing is left but a soft green color, the color of a spring forest. . . .

Now is a time of rest. Feel your body rest. There is nothing you must do in this protected time and space—only rest. Your muscles are becoming increasingly heavy, pleasantly heavy. . . . Your eyelids are becoming heavy. . . . In this quiet, comfortable place, your thoughts flow by like driftwood down a lazy, winding river. When a thought comes to you, say to yourself: There goes another thought. Let the thought drift by on the lazy river as you breathe comfortably and deeply. . . .

If there is any tension, pain, or distress in your body, breathe long, healing breaths through that spot in your body. Each breath is cool and soothing. Breathe until all you are aware of is comfort and soothing. . . .

Enjoy letting your unconscious mind, where God often walks, show you how relaxed you are. . . .

Continue relaxing now for as long as you like. Your mind, spirit, and body are one. You are now open to change and imagination. . . . Let God speak to you as the veil drops between your busy, surface mind and your deep, quiet unconscious mind. . . .

From this point you may proceed to any exercise that uses your imagination.

2

Journaling

to Recover

from Addiction

The Roots of Addiction

The roots of addiction, dysfunction, and co-dependence grow very deep. Addicts are deeply wounded at a young age. Dysfunctional families are always turned upside down—they never seem to offer enough nourishment for healthy emotional growth. Instead of receiving enough love, children in dysfunctional families experience too much fear; instead of mom or dad taking care of the children, the children are left too much alone to care for themselves, often becoming parents to their own mothers and fathers. Such early childhood wounding freezes emotional growth under a thick layer of shame. Shame comes from never having enough emotional nourishment to become healthy adults. In the adult addict, the body and intellect mature, but the spirit and psyche remain frozen in dysfunctional childhood. The following story tells what addiction feels like—living in a grown-up body with the psyche of a child.

A Horse and His Man

Once upon a time, there was a horse who rode a man. Neither the man nor the horse knew any better. That's the way they both thought life should be. When they first began to travel together, they were very young. But as the horse grew bigger than the man with each passing year, riding became an exhausting experience

23

for both of them. The man with the huge horse on his back moved very slowly. The horse often lost its balance and sat on the man's head, forcing him into the mud. With mud in his eyes, the man lost his sense of direction. So the man and the horse spent years traveling around in circles, coming back to the same starting place again and again and again.

A normal child's behavioral impulses are like the horse. Impulsivity in a child is charming. We laugh at high-spirited children and enjoy their spontaneity. But the same childish, impulsive behaviors in adults are not at all charming. Addictive impulses and behaviors of the wounded inner child drive an adult addict. Impulsive, childish urges constantly remind the addict that there will never be enough of anything in life. Only abusing a substance or a relationship will nourish the old, inner childhood hunger. So the horse rides the adult in hopeless, addictive circles.

Our conscious minds forget childhood wounds, but our bodies remember. Often the roots of addiction occur much earlier than we consciously remember. The childhood emotional processes that launched us on our circular journeys of addiction usually remain frozen behind walls of shame. While our minds cannot penetrate these walls, our bodies mindlessly act out addictive impulses in futile attempts to medicate the shame, heal old wounds, and feed that gnawing childish hunger.

In order to get our horses off our backs, we need to wed those old, childish impulses to words. We must learn to verbalize what we need for recovery. The written word helps us examine old, addictive impulses before we mindlessly act on them. When we learn to write about our addictive impulses, we learn to ride the horse at last.

Journaling Is Critical to Recovery

Writing about your addictive process slows you down so you can make choices about your behavior and use language to ask for what you need from the world. Journaling in recovery returns control to your life.

An addict is someone out of control. If you are an addict or codependent, you know what it is like to be obsessed with a substance, activity, or relationship. Your obsession consumed all of your time, attention, and energy until you lost all control over your life. Journaling your recovery returns your life to you. Writing about your experience of addiction or co-dependence gives you the gift of words to describe that inner experience of longing and craving. Persistent journaling replaces impulsive behavior with mature reflection.

When you give words to your internal needs, slowly you learn to fulfill those needs in a healthy way, rather than relying on old, destructive patterns of addiction. Learning to meet your needs in ways that promote growth and maturity is fun and exciting. But the struggle to shape words out of childish impulses requires work and patience. Finding words for infant impulses and primitive reactions is slow work. *Tracks in the Sand* will help you experiment and practice putting words to impulsive feelings and urges as you write about them in your journal. Journaling helps you build a healthy relationship with yourself. Practice is also needed in using words to form healthy emotional relationships with others. A Twelve Step, Overcomers Outreach, support, or therapy group will help you build healthy relationships with the outside world. Writing in your journal is most helpful when combined with continuing involvement in a recovery group.

Guidelines for Journaling in Recovery

You continue your recovery by writing in your journal daily. This workbook will guide you through a series of structured journaling exercises designed to help you recover a healthy, growing emotional life.

When recording the events and activities of the day, it is extremely important to write about the thoughts and feelings that went with your activities and relationships. Remember, you are learning a new, reflective way of being in the world. You are learning to slow down in order to contain the internal urge to indulge addictive impulses. When recording your daily life in your journal, the more you write about your everyday feelings, no matter how small, the deeper your recovery will be. Write those addictive impulses on the pages of your journal. Write about the desire to use a substance or abuse a relationship. Describe in detail your emotional reactions to the events and people in your day. Recording such moments in your day may seem small and petty, but such a record is crucial to your recovery.

For example, you may write about your emotional reaction to a cutting remark by a co-worker; or write about how you felt when you asked for love and he or she just looked the other way; or you may want to write about never getting enough recognition on the job. You may find yourself thinking: Don't be so petty! Grow up! Blow it off! But then the desire to act on your addictive impulse sneaks up behind you while you are busy telling yourself it doesn't matter. Instead, ask yourself how these seemingly trivial instances contribute to your impulse to use a substance, abuse a relationship, or get down on yourself. Use your journal to explore alternative behaviors in response to such small moments in life. Keeping a daily journal of your thoughts and feelings helps you identify, examine, and trace addictive impulses, instead of thoughtlessly acting on them.

Also remember to write about your daily victories in life. Being in recovery is about recovering joy in life. If it is critical to record your reactions and impulses to the painful moments of your day, it is even more important to capture moments of joy in your journal. Write about those daily situations when you were proud of yourself; or the happiness that comes from loving without being co-dependent; or the deep satisfaction of living one more day clean and sober. Recording little moments of pleasure and happiness encourages you to continue in recovery, and helps you experience recovery as the most exciting journey of your life.

Everything You Don't Feel, You Steal

Theft occurs when you act on an addictive impulse. You steal a drink; or make a co-dependent rescue; or go on an eating binge. When your internal security system is down, the thieving impulse steals your life from you.

Theft occurs when you don't allow yourself to take pleasure in the moments of joy life offers. The serenity that comes from being alive and clean is stolen from you when you don't slow down long enough to enjoy life.

Journaling is part of the internal security system that monitors addictive impulses and captures fleeting moments of joy. The structured journaling exercises that follow help you identify those issues that often appear repeatedly throughout recovery. You may return to these exercises again and again to explore the joy of recovery.

Before you complete a new exercise, or make a new entry in your journal, read over the last entry you made. We quickly forget the lessons we've learned, or the satisfaction that comes from our small victories. The habit of going around and around in muddy circles is so deep in us any other new, alternative route feels strange and scary until we begin to see the new path in front of us. Your journal is like a priceless mirror—you need to see your self again and again before you begin to believe someone is really there at all. There is beauty and hope in the act of re-reading yourself in your journal. By reading and re-reading your journal, you will begin to see the growth of an internal parent who affirms you, loves you, and walks with you on your recovery journey.

This exercise will help you bring healing and hope to the small, but sometimes powerful part of you who threatens failure and a return to old, addictive patterns. This exercise refers to this part of you as your "failed self," often experienced as your wounded, childhood self. You may have first really experienced the power of your failed self when you bottomed out in your addiction. Your failed self, your wounded inner child, is a small part of you who remains with you even in recovery.

As you begin this exercise, remember that your failed self is only a tiny part of your total self. You may have failed in your life, but you are much, much more than failure. You are a believer in God, a friend, a family member, an employee—and still you are more than the sum of all of these parts! In this exercise you will discover the wounded inner child you carry with you. But you are not that wounded child all the time. This exercise will offer you the opportunity to care for and nourish your failed self that is so often your inner child.

Exercise

Choose an object from your environment that represents your failed self. Simply walk around the house or garden and pick up an object into which you will put your failed self, your wounded inner child, during this exercise. This object may be any one of a number of things—a figurine or small statue; a pack of matches; a dried flower; a burned out light bulb; pruning shears or scissors; a photograph of you as a child; soil from the garden; an empty jar or glass. Take about fifteen minutes or so and explore the house or garden until you find an object that seems to fit this part of you. Bring the object back to the place where you will be writing in your journal.

Set the object in front of you on a table or on the floor in front of your chair. Then open your journal. Look closely at the object in front of you. Imagine your failed self somewhere inside the object. Now choose a name for the object and the failed self it holds. The name you choose may be a childhood nickname that picked on a weakness of yours, like Skinny, Dummy, Fatty, and so forth. Or you may choose a name that describes how your failed self feels—for example, Mr. Hungry, Miss Lonelyhearts, Burned Out, or D. Pressed.

Once you have named the failed self living in the object, write a letter in your journal to this part of you. In the first part of this letter record the series of failures this wounded part of you has caused in your life that eventually led to your addiction. Along with each failure, write down the thoughts and feelings that accompanied each event. For example:

> *Dear Chicken,*
>
> *I remember the day you got that drunk driving ticket. You'd just had that fight with your wife and were feeling angry inside. And now you remind me of all those fights Mom and Dad used to have, and how you were scared and helpless. It was then you started drinking. . . .*

To begin the second part of the letter to your failed self, write with understanding and love, especially love. Use words you would have liked to hear from your own parents, words you wanted spoken to you when you were little, hurt, frightened, or embarrassed. Tell your failed self, your wounded inner child, that you understand and offer healing on this recovery journey. When you have finished the second part of the letter, sign and date it.

Now imagine you as your failed self, locked in the object in front of you. Write a letter in your journal from your failed self in response to the first letter. Use your non-dominant hand to write this response.

When writing a letter as your failed self, write whatever you may be feeling inside after having received and read the first letter. For example, you may be angry at having been ignored for so long; you may feel sad and ashamed at all the failures you've caused; or you may feel happy and relieved that you are finally getting some compassionate attention. You may want to write about how you would like to be treated differently in the future. You may even wish to be called by a different name. Use this letter to make your existence known. When you have finished writing the letter from your failed self, sign and date it.

Put away your journal for now. Return the object to its place.

Encouraging the Discouraged Self

Beginning to love your self is a big step. Don't expect to do it perfectly all at once. Loving your self takes patience and practice. Simply *trying* to love your self is a mark of improvement. But be prepared for setbacks. Recovering addicts become discouraged easily. You need continuous encouragement to keep on the recovery path you have chosen.

Addicts and co-dependents are used to getting encouragement from a substance, activity, or relationship. When we get frustrated, we seek comfort in alcohol, food, chemicals, or inappropriate relationships. Now the challenge is to get the same encouragement and comfort from within ourselves rather than the outside world. Getting such encouragement and comfort comes from the process of growing loving parents inside ourselves. These interior, caring parents are our inner support systems, from whom encouragement and comfort are always available.

There is a biblical support system available to us in the book of Hebrews. In Hebrews 12:1, we are told there is a great cloud of witnesses always watching over us and encouraging us. These people knew discouragement. They often failed. And yet they were counted among the faithful. The people listed in chapter 11 of Hebrews, as well as all of the angels and the Lord God himself, are all rooting for you in your struggle to overcome your addiction! Chapter 11 of Hebrews is a good place to begin shopping for an inner parent, someone you carry inside to support and encourage you in your recovery.

Exercise

Get out your Bible. Read Hebrews 11:1 through 12:14. When you have finished reading, close your Bible and close your eyes. Imagine yourself seated among this great cloud of witnesses, this circle of spiritual encouragers. You are surrounded by people from all the ages, the angels, and God. You know they are all watching you from a heavenly grandstand as your life unfolds on Earth. Each failure from you brings a sympathetic groan from each of them. Each act of restraint or faith brings a roar of praise. These many witnesses of your life, as well as your Heavenly Parent, want you to take them inside yourself. They want to become your inner support system and function as loving, caring parents different from the ones you were given at birth. They promise love, nourishment, and healthy discipline that will enable you to heal, grow, and flourish.

Slowly open your eyes and open your journal. Write what it felt like to be in this circle of heavenly supporters. Include what you saw, heard, and felt. Give words to what you wanted to say to these people, to the angels, and to God. If you found it difficult to join the heavenly support group, write about how hard it was for you. When you have recorded your experience fully, close your journal and take a fifteen minute break before continuing the exercise.

Open your journal again and write a letter to yourself from one of your heavenly supporters. Choose one person with whom you most identify from the list of heroes and heroines in Hebrews 11. Pretend you are the hero or heroine you have selected. Write a letter to your failed self again, only this time it is from the vantage point of this biblical person. If you cannot identify with any of the people from the Hebrews' passage, choose someone from your own past who was an important source of encouragement and nurture. The letter your encourager is about to write must communicate support and firmness.

For example, such a letter might read:

Hi! I'm Moses. Even though I was a murderer, God used me to liberate my people from slavery. I know what it is like to be a slave and so do you. You never need go back into slavery again because I know you love God. Don't give in to those urges to indulge your addiction. God has better plans for you than that. Trust God to help you work your recovery. I, Moses, a former slave, will be here for you to remind you of the power of God to liberate you.

When you have finished this letter, write a letter back to your heavenly supporter. Let this letter come from your heart, from the failed self who is always afraid of blowing it. Use your non-dominant hand when writing this response. Let your heavenly supporter know how you are doing, the doubts you may have about staying sober, or the desperate feelings you have when you try to change your co-dependent behavior.

After you have finished your return letter, close your eyes and imagine hearing words of encouragement from your heavenly supporter. Let your self feel comforted and soothed. Hear the words of gentle, firm discipline that communicate genuine love and caring.

Open your eyes and jot in your journal the words of encouragement you heard. If you choose, you may close by inviting your heavenly supporter to become your inner, loving parent to journey with you in recovery.

The Internal Father

You are now on your way toward growing a nurturing, loving inner parent who offers support, encouragement, and comfort for recovery. When growing a new, loving interior parent for recovery, it is important to be aware of the inner father you have unconsciously carried inside you since childhood. This inner father may be a source of strength who offers support as you learn to re-parent yourself; or your inner father may be a voice that continually attempts to thwart and obstruct your recovery journey; or your inner father may be a confusing mixture of strengths and weaknesses. Father is a powerful figure whose voice continues to influence your recovery for good or for ill.

This next section examines your father—your external father, the one you were born with, and the father you learned to carry around inside you at an early age—your inner father who is still with you today.

A common experience among addictive personalities is a weak connection with their fathers. In dysfunctional families, father was often a negative influence on his children—he was overly critical; he was often abusive; and may even have been an addict himself. Sometimes father contributed to his family's dysfunction by being either emotionally or physically absent—he was away at work or simply never at home; he rarely demonstrated love and acceptance toward other family members; or he didn't protect his children from their dysfunctional or addicted mother. The result of such negative fatherly influence is that the children often build a negative internal image of father. Children who grow up in dysfunctional families often carry inside them a frightening or incomplete internal father who continues to dwell with them into adulthood.

Such a negative internal father is either too weak to help you control your addictive cravings, or he actively contributes to your addictive impulses. Therefore, you must get to know the inner father you carry with you on your recovery journey. The following exercise is designed to help you learn to consciously listen to your father's voice and begin to develop a positive internal father figure for recovery.

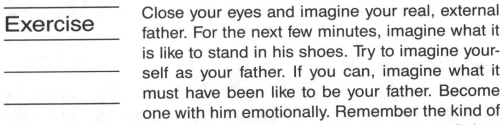

Exercise

Close your eyes and imagine your real, external father. For the next few minutes, imagine what it is like to stand in his shoes. Try to imagine yourself as your father. If you can, imagine what it must have been like to be your father. Become one with him emotionally. Remember the kind of family in which he grew up. For a little while, you are now your father.

Open your eyes and your journal. Write a letter from your father to you, the child who grew up to become an addict. Use your non-dominant hand as your internal father writes his letter to you, your conscious self. Allow your internal father to write honestly. If imagining father is difficult for you, guess at what he might want to write to you.

When your internal father has finished writing, put the pen in your dominant hand and write a letter back to him. Write any negative feelings you may have toward him—anger, contempt, guilt, and so on. Then write about any feelings of grief or longing you may have regarding him—father hunger, sadness, a sense of loss, and so forth. Finally, if you can, summon any love you may still have for him and close your letter with that. Be sure to close and sign your letter.

Now close your journal and take a fifteen minute break. When you've finished your break, open your journal and re-read the letters. Scan the letters for any positive, nurturing qualities you want to bestow on your new internal parent. If you have difficulty finding loving fatherly qualities in your letters, imagine positive qualities you would have liked to experience from your father. Briefly list those qualities in your journal. As you continue to grow your encouraging, supportive, internal parent, consult this list for clues and messages and feelings of comfort your new parent may give you for your recovery.

Healing the Shamed Self

You have examined your failed self and the importance of growing a positive, nurturing, internal parent who assists you in healing the failed self. Now you will explore the experience of shame, an emotion that underlies all feelings of failure. You will learn to call on your loving inner parent to begin to heal the part of you who always feels ashamed.

When we have been in recovery long enough, we begin to feel our emotions again. The anesthetic numbness that comes from abusing substances and relationships wears off, and the feelings we've been avoiding and medicating re-enter our daily lives. One overwhelming emotion that begins to surface is the feeling of shame. Shame is often at the root of many other feelings. John Bradshaw calls shame "the master emotion."[1] The Bible uses the word for shame three times more often than the word for guilt. Addicts and co-dependents are intimately familiar with the experience of shame.

Shame acts as an amplifier for other powerful, negative emotions. It is often the hidden catalyst that transforms these negative emotions into actions. For example, shame mixed with a deep longing or sense of inadequacy produces addictive behavior. The addictive impulses and behaviors serve to cover up shame, suppress it, numb its power and feeling. The life of an addict is one of continually acting out addictive impulses to avoid feeling the pain of shame.

Shame not only transforms negative emotions into addictive behavior, it is also addictive itself. Addicts and co-dependents become so used to living with shame, suppressing it and avoiding it, they become addicted to behaviors and relationships that never help them confront and heal their shame. In a way, shame becomes the hidden, familiar, addictive high. We most often court the unpleasantly familiar at the expense of the pleasantly unfamiliar. It is easier to continue to abuse relationships and substances, to continue to deny the power of shame in our lives, than to bring our shame out into the healing process of recovery.

The following exercise is designed to help you identify the shame you carry with you and to enlist the healing support of your internal parent in bringing your shame into recovery.

Exercise

Close your eyes for a moment and remember a time recently when you felt ashamed. Ask yourself: What did shame feel like in your body? Did you blush, look away, become suddenly jovial, want to run and hide? Once you are able to locate where in your body you feel shame, open your journal and briefly record your physical experience of shame. Here is an excerpt from my journal to guide you:

Whenever I am ashamed and I'm with you, I glance down and away from you. I tighten my jaw, tense my shoulders slightly, and my breathing gets very shallow. I begin to fidget with my fingers. I feel an impulse to get busy with some activity, or suddenly decide to get something to eat or drink.

Your physical experience of shame may be different from mine, but locate the experience of shame in your body. When you have finished writing about your body and its experience of shame, take a five minute break.

The next part of this exercise requires a little preparation before you can begin. You are going to draw an image of a common object in or around your house, such as a flower, a tree, the couch, a lamp, or a vase. Choose an object you would enjoy working on, but is fairly easy to do. Decide whether you want to draw a picture in your journal or make a sketch using drawing paper. To draw or sketch the object, you will need to assemble either a number two pencil, or a variety of colored pens, pencils, or crayons, and a sketching pad or blank paper (if you want to make your drawing outside your journal). When you have assembled the items you need, and have selected an object to draw, you are ready to begin the exercise.

Exercise

Using your non-dominant hand, begin to sketch or draw a picture of the object you have chosen. As you work, pay attention to any awakened memories, mental images, and self-talk that accompany the act of drawing. Especially notice any feelings that surface as you draw.

When you have finished drawing, open your journal. Record any memories, mental images, self-talk, or feelings the drawing exercise awakened in you. Now look carefully at your drawing, and write your feelings about it. Does the voice of your inner critic make you ashamed of your effort? Did making this sketch awaken any other feelings or messages of shame and embarrassment? If so, spend a few minutes writing about that.

Look again at your drawing. Examine it carefully. Ask your nurturing inner parent to look through your eyes at your drawing, and tell you what he or she likes about it. Listen carefully for the answer. Write in your journal two things your inner parent especially liked about your sketch. Then fold your drawing and put it in your journal. Close your journal for now.

You may not remember specific times during your childhood when you experienced shame. But your body remembers. Your body has locked in its tissues all the times you experienced shame. Locating the physical presence of shame in your body brings a healing awareness. Often doing something creative unlocks the voices, memories, and feelings of shame that continue with us as adults. When you are aware of how you continue to shame yourself, you may always enlist the support and comfort of your inner parent in easing the sense of shame you learned too well. So, notice your body when you are ashamed. Let yourself be creative with your body—do more drawing, work with modeling clay, fingerpaint—and listen for the voices that still make you ashamed. And always call on your loving inner parent to counteract those negative voices of shame.

What to Do When You Can't Get Enough

Another core emotion underlying much addictive behavior is a persistent fear that there is never enough of whatever is necessary to meet our needs. This fear may be experienced in a variety of ways: there is never enough love; never enough security; never enough money; never enough happiness; never enough excitement; and so on. This fear of never getting enough produces a lot of painful stress in our lives. Addicts and co-dependents are good at experiencing stress and terrible at experiencing comfort. We have learned from childhood there is never enough of anything. As adults, our wounded inner child is always crying, "MORE!" And we end up using substances and abusing relationships in futile attempts to hush the cries for more.

The following story and journaling exercise are designed to help you get in touch with the part of your self that never gets enough. Having done that, you will discover there is enough, and more than enough, in the world and in your self to meet your needs.

A Prince's Journey

Once upon a time, there was a son who lived in the castle of his father, the king. One day the young prince went to his father and asked to go traveling into the world to discover his fate. The father equipped him with a horse, a dog, weapons, and armor.

The young man traveled deep into the forest for many days and nights. One day he came to a deep blue, perfectly round lake surrounded by a sandy beach. The prince tethered his horse, climbed a tree with his dog, and waited. After a while he grew thirsty. So he climbed back down the tree and scooped up a handful of water for himself and his dog, and went back up the tree to wait.

Soon a huge, moaning giantess who was missing half her body, limped over a hill. She dragged herself to the water's edge and drank and drank the water until the lake was dry. Fish flopped in the empty basin. Then the half-giantess began to wail. She beat the earth with her fists and thundered, "THERE IS NOT ENOUGH!! MY THIRST IS UNQUENCHED!!" The ground shook with her pounding and wailing. Finally, she exhausted herself and slept. When she awoke, she dragged herself back the way she had come.

The prince came down from the tree and followed her at a distance. She led him to her castle and the young man hid and spied on her. She lit a fire under an enormous cauldron in front of the drawbridge. The incomplete, but powerful giantess saw a herd of buffalo wander by the castle and she scooped up a dozen of them in her huge hands, tore them limb from limb, and threw them into her cauldron. A flock of geese flew overhead. The half-giantess reached up and caught a dozen geese, tore them to shreds, and threw them into her cauldron. Then she added a hundred bags of flour, barley, peas, and oats. While the stew cooked, the giantess went in the castle to prepare herself for dinner.

Meanwhile, the son of the king was hidden in a tree near the cauldron. When the giantess left, he speared a piece of meat for himself and his dog, then hid himself again in the branches of the tree.

When the half-giantess returned, she tipped the cauldron to her mouth and swallowed the entire stew. She looked at the bottom of the pot and began to scream, "THERE IS NOT ENOUGH!" She raged, breathed fire, and stomped the ground. After a time of ranting and raving, the half-giantess exhausted herself and, once again, she slept. As she slept, the prince made a stealthy, speedy retreat.

He rode back over the many miles to his father's castle. He rode over the drawbridge, into the main hall, and right up to the king's throne. He dismounted his horse and removed his armor. The king, amazed at the changes in his son, rushed to embrace him. At his father's touch, the son said, "Father, I have seen life."

Exercise

Choose the detail of the story that most grabbed your attention. You may choose a person, animal, event, speech, or part of the landscape. Whatever detail you choose will serve as your doorway into the story.

Open your journal. Become the detail you chose from the story and write in the first person. Pretend you are actually a piece of the story. Here are a few examples of how to begin:

I am the half-giantess. I am slurping down the stew . . .

I am the dog. I am afraid for my master—he is obsessed with this giantess . . .

I am a tree. I offer a place to hide until it is safe to come out . . .

I am the lake. I don't like the giantess drinking all of me. There is not enough of me for everyone . . .

Spend about fifteen minutes writing the piece of the story you've chosen.

Record any feelings you had that went with being in the story. Were you frightened, brave, sad, confused?

Finally, spend about fifteen minutes writing any connections you may see between the detail you chose, the feelings that went with it, and your fear of never having enough. For example:

The piece of the story that grabbed my attention was the prince hidden in the tree near the giantess' cauldron. I was afraid I might fall in the cauldron and become part of the stew. Her consuming rage was terrifying. I associated my own addiction to speed, of moving too fast through life, with running from this giantess. I'm still running from this giantess in the following ways . . .

Now close your journal for a few moments and close your eyes. Repeat these words to yourself three times:

There is enough, and more than enough, in Christ, my Savior.

Open your journal to a blank page and label the top, "Times this week when I got enough of what I needed." Throughout the coming week, return to this page and record each time you experienced having enough to meet your needs. For example, your list could begin to look like this:

1. *Having coffee with Susan filled my need for friendship today.*
2. *Being thanked for doing a good job filled my need for recognition today.*
3. *Holding hands with John filled my need for support today.*
4. *Taking a hot bubble bath filled my need for nurturing today.*

Spending a week recording those times when you experience getting enough shows your ability to continue on your journey of recovery. It also helps you practice getting what you need when the fear of never having enough raises its ugly head.

When you have completed your list for the week, thank God for the ways he helped you fulfill your needs.

Healing the Unrecovered Self

There are small, sometimes powerful parts of ourselves that continue to fight recovery. We have already explored a few of them: the failed self, the hidden corners of ourselves that still experience the sting of shame, and the perpetually hungry self, who fears never having enough. There may still be lurking inside you a part of yourself who remains unrecovered, who continues to sabotage your best efforts to find healing.

The following story and journaling exercise are designed to help you identify any other stubborn part of you who fears traveling the path of recovery. Once you identify the frightened part of you who resists recovery, you can give voice to the fear, understand what that part of you needs, and lovingly invite it to join with your family of self on the road to recovery.

The Bird and the Blackened Branch

Once upon a time, a forest fire burned to the ground a section of live oaks growing near a lake. A bare, black stump with a single charred branch was all that was left of the oaks. This branch held a robin's nest. The robin and her babies survived the fire because the branch hung over the lake.

One fine spring day, the mother robin herded her three little fledglings to the end of the blackened branch. She advanced menacingly on them, pushing them away from the charred nest and tree, the only world the babies had ever known. Terrified, two of the baby birds jumped off the branch and plunged toward the water. Just before they fell into the lake, their little wings began to beat, and they began to fly.

The third little fledgling was too frightened to let go of the branch. The mother robin stalked toward him, waving her wings and chirping loudly, but the baby bird dug his claws into the very end of the branch. The mother gave her baby a big shove, and the little bird swung underneath the branch, his little claws still hanging on for dear life. The determined mother robin pecked at her baby's little claws. At last, the baby robin let go. He fell headlong toward the water. But just before he fell into the lake, his little wings began to beat, and he started to fly.

Exercise

Open your journal. Write how you feel about the baby bird who wouldn't let go, who refused to explore what lay beyond a charred nest and a burned-out tree. You may want to answer the following questions to help you get started: Who is the part of you that is the baby robin hanging on to the blackened branch? How does that frightened part of you express itself in your body?

When you look inside your self, you may not see a frightened baby bird. Another image of this part of your self may come to mind. If so, describe this minority part in your family of self, this hanger-on, this dreamer, this believer of addictive illusions. Use as much detail as possible in describing this part of your unrecovered self. Then write as your unrecovered self in the first person. Describe how it feels to be the one holding on for dear life to the patterns of addiction.

Now write a dialogue between your unrecovered self and the conscious part of you who is pushing to change, who is excited about recovery, and delighted with the adventure of it all. Continue to write the dialogue until you feel both parts of you have said all they need to say for now. Close the dialogue by gently, lovingly inviting your unrecovered self to journey down the road to recovery for a while. Then close your journal and put it away.

You will always carry a resistant, unrecovered part of you on your journey of recovery. Return to this exercise whenever you feel there is a part of you refusing to change and grow. Whenever possible help the conscious part of you, who always pushes and pushes for change, to listen to and understand your frightened, unrecovered self. Show your frightened self gentleness and compassion so that your recovery will bring deep and lasting change.

Summary

You have explored how journaling helps expose the roots of addiction and speeds you on your journey of recovery. There is much power in giving words to your failed, shamed, and unrecovered self. You have also begun to grow your nurturing inner parent who guides you on your journey to recovery.

Other chapters in this book help you to journal about various aspects of the recovery process. As you read the other chapters and work the exercises, remember to enjoy the adventure of discovery in recovery.

3

Recovering

from Depression

Through Journaling

Depression: A Crisis of Growth

When we work a recovery program successfully, invariably we experience feelings of sadness or depression. Such feelings are not a sign of failure in recovery, for when we begin to feel sad or depressed, we are no longer medicating the pain by abusing a substance or a relationship. In the beginning of recovery, some of the sadness may result from mourning the loss of our addictions. Feelings of depression, then, are often a sign of growth in recovery.

Part of the work of recovery is developing an inner container that will hold all our newly discovered emotions. In the early stages of recovery our containers were not sufficiently developed to hold all of our new, non-medicated thoughts and feelings. Often those feelings of sadness or depression seemed to leak out into the world. Our internal selves, or containers, just weren't strong enough yet to tolerate temporary bouts of depression and sadness. We were tempted to medicate the depression or engage in co-dependent behavior to divert our attention from the sadness. But as we progressed in recovery, and our internal containers became stronger, we learned to allow ourselves to experience feelings that come with depression. And we learned how to make positive choices in handling this crisis of growth.

We continue to progress in our recovery by giving up old, destructive behavior patterns and learning new skills. Whenever we let go of old behavior patterns, feelings of depression are frequently the result. Until we learn new, healthier ways of living, we often feel sad over the loss of our old, unhealthy lifestyles. Therefore, occasional bouts of depression are the litmus test of true recovery.

However, we need to focus a moment on deep, lasting depression. Some people enter a profound, chronic or long-lasting depression. Sometimes this serious form of depression is accompanied by thoughts of suicide. Should this kind of deep depression ever be a part of your experience, seek immediate professional help from a licensed mental health professional. The help of such a professional can be literally life-giving. The causes of severe depression are many and varied, but it does *not* mean you have somehow failed in your recovery. This chapter does not explore such deep experiences of depression. Prolonged depression requires specific guidance from a therapist.

The kind of depression this chapter explores is a temporary experience, indicating an opportunity for growth in your recovery. When encountering depression in recovery, you have an opportunity to take a giant step forward.

Weathering the storm of depression is like suddenly stepping into a bright, spring day. If depression feels like a kind of death, coming out on the other side of sadness and loss is like resurrection. Another world opens up, a quality of living the great psychologist Abraham Maslow called "postmortem life." Authors Feinstein and Krippner paint a breathtaking picture of what life is like on the other side of sadness:

> Everything gets doubly precious, gets piercingly important. You get stabbed by things, by flowers and by babies and by beautiful things—just the very act of living, of walking and breathing and eating and having friends and chatting. Everything seems to look more beautiful rather than less, and one gets the much intensified sense of miracles. . . . Everything looks so precious, so sacred, so beautiful that I feel more strongly than ever the impulse to love it, to embrace it, and to let myself be overwhelmed by it.[1]

Recovering Hope Again

A man named G. Bok said, "If I had a thing to give you, I would tell you one more time that the world is always turning toward the morning."

When you are depressed, the world seems always to turn toward night. You feel in your bones that the darkest hour is just before midnight. In your depression you have learned to carry a heavy load of sadness, loneliness, and grief. But there is another skill that can be learned in the darkness of depression. In her book *And the Trees Clap Their Hands*, Virginia Stem Owens writes about developing the skill of giving thanks during dark, hard times:

> If you go poking about in the world, intent on keeping the candle of consciousness blazing, you must be ready to give thanks at all times. Discrimination is not allowed. The flame cannot gutter and fail when a cold wind whistles throughout the house.
>
> Thanksgiving is not a task to be undertaken lightly. It is not for dilettantes or aesthetes. One does not dabble in praise for one's own amusement. . . . We're not talking about the world as a free course in art appreciation. No. Thanksgiving is not a result of perception; thanksgiving is the access to perception.[2]

Thanksgiving is also the path to recovering hope. An old saying in the recovery movement is "fake it till you make it." The idea is if you act cheerfully, you will feel cheerful. I'd like to change that saying to "stake it till you claim it." Stake your inner claim on hope through faith in God and hold on to that hope in your outer life.

Stare into the night and believe in the sunrise. The Bible calls this the sacrifice of praise (Hebrews 13:15). The Scriptures are full of stories about staking and claiming hope in the midst of depressing circumstances. Consider the following examples.

A young man, the night before he knew he was to be executed, broke bread at his last supper. He knew this represented his body to be broken, and yet he gave thanks. He looked into the cup, knowing it represented his own blood to be spilled, and still he gave thanks. Jesus left the dinner table and walked to Gethsemane. He knew he would be arrested there, but while he walked, he sang a hymn and gave thanks (see Luke 22).

The apostle Paul was in prison, his back raw from being beaten. It was midnight. Paul and his friend Silas began to sing praises to God. An earthquake rocked the prison as they sang, and they were set free (see Acts 16).

The prophet Jonah was swallowed by a big fish. While clinging to the ribs of the fish, his head wrapped in seaweed, Jonah offered praise to God. The Lord spoke to the fish, who spat Jonah on dry land (see Jonah 2).

Israel was surrounded and outnumbered by enemies. Their destruction was eminent. Then they did a crazy thing. They organized a choir and began to sing praises to God. Their enemies began fighting among themselves and wiped themselves out (see 2 Chronicles 20).

David was being chased as a common outlaw by the king. He was in hiding for years. While hiding out, David wrote many of the Psalms, the world's most praise-filled literature.

The prophet Habakkuk was a farmer. His crop failed, and his animals were killed. He lost everything. But in the middle of these disasters, he thanked God (see Habakkuk 3:16–19).

All these people had problems. They stared death, suffering, and loss in the face. They felt the fullness of their grief. They offered up their sacrifices of praise to God because their choices were limited and their relationship with God merited such action.

These people in the Bible are like you—depression was often their lot in life. It was when their backs were to the wall that they chose to stake their claim on giving thanks and praise to the God they loved.

The following exercise will help you give thanks. It is critical to recovery that thanksgiving become a habit. Return to this exercise again and again for inspiration in making thanksgiving and praise a part of your routine, especially during times of depression.

Exercise

Put on some music that inspires your heart to praise and thank God. Make sure your tape player, compact disc player, or record player is in a private place. Sing out loud or hum along with the music. As you listen or sing, close your eyes and imagine the music piercing the darkness, the sadness of your depression, and lighting your soul with the presence of God. Spend at least fifteen minutes listening, singing, and experiencing God's presence.

While the music continues to play, open your eyes and open your journal. You may express your thanks or give praise to God using your journal in three different ways. Write God a thank-you letter. Thank him for whatever good may come out of your loss, even though you may be unable to see any goodness just now. Thank God that he shares in your present suffering. Thank God for not rescuing you from the fiery furnace of your depression; praise him for entering the fire to be with you, even though he may remain invisible.

Or write your own psalm to God. Should you decide to write a psalm, include how you feel in the midst of your depression, how you experience God's presence or absence, and close with an expression of thanks and praise.

If you find that words simply will not come, draw a picture or sketch in your journal that expresses your thanks through the pain.

You may find that giving thanks and praise in the midst of your depression is something you just cannot do right now. Instead you may find you need to rage and storm, to cry or even sulk at God and those who have hurt you before you can do this exercise. Or you may find you need first to spend some time with a friend, sponsor, or therapist who will warm you with encouragement and understanding. Whatever the reason, if you cannot complete this exercise now, do not do it. It is okay to skip it for now and come back to it at another time. Be patient with yourself; God is not ashamed of you right now, so you do not need to shame yourself into finishing the exercise. It will be here for you whenever you feel ready to use it.

After writing or sketching your thanks and praise, close your journal. If time and opportunity permit, let the music continue to play while you do other things.

Recovering hope in the midst of depression means beginning a routine of expressing thanks and praise to God. Being grateful when you don't feel like it is very hard work. One summer I was overwhelmed with depression after experiencing a significant loss. I made a practice of swimming laps in a pool, crying and singing over and over, "The joy of the Lord is my strength!" But it was very hard to do. Writing is helpful, too, though it isn't always easy. When you express your gratitude to God regularly over time in your journal, you may find your depression slowly lifts, and you have begun the long, hard-won process of recovering hope.

Journaling and Depression

Recovering from addiction and co-dependency is learning to slow down enough to feel and tolerate pain, instead of anesthetizing the pain by abusing a substance or relationship. Recovering from depression is mobilizing our bodies to express the pain we feel. Depression has a way of immobilizing our bodies. We get stuck in a drifting, lifeless place, without any energy, and we feel helpless to help ourselves. Journaling mobilizes our bodies. The simple act of picking up a pen or pencil and writing a few lines in a journal is movement—it energizes our bodies and encourages us to take a step forward in recovery.

Clinical experience with people suffering depression shows that learning a new skill is critical in recovering from depression. The following exercises are designed to help you build new skills in coping with depression. Before beginning the exercises, remember to *be kind to yourself.* When you are depressed, it is very hard to summon the physical energy to do anything at all, even writing seems to take a lot of effort. Therefore, after you complete every exercise in this chapter, reward yourself with a favorite treat: Take yourself out to dinner or see a movie with a friend. Chat on the phone with your sponsor or a loved one who lives too far away to visit. Take a hot bubble bath. Snuggle up with a good book. Plan a long walk with someone you love. Showing simple kindness to yourself in the middle of depression is vital to recovery.

Loss and Mourning

When you are depressed, it often means you have experienced a loss. Most of the time it is related to the loss of something or someone. It may be a friendship has ended; a relative has died; you've lost your job or made a career change; or your health is poor. Or it may be that you are only now beginning to experience a loss that happened a long, long time ago. Whether your loss is recent or happened in the past, you feel an emptiness inside that nothing, or no one, seems able to fill. Often that emptiness is experienced as depression.

You must identify and experience loss to recover from depression.

The following exercise will help you name and claim the losses you have experienced. Naming each loss helps you to identify them. After naming each one, claim those that cause your present depression. Claiming your losses means you are no longer in denial about the impact they still have on your life. Once you have claimed your losses, you are able to mourn them and continue your recovery.

Exercise

Open your journal. The first part of this exercise is naming your losses. In ten minutes, on the left side of your journal page list as many losses as you can. Don't try to think about them—just name them. The losses may be big or small; they can come from your long ago past or have happened only yesterday. Your list might include old sweethearts; school failures; death; physical illness or injury; divorce; disappointed hopes; and so forth. Name each loss using only a few words. For example:

Broken engagement with John.
Mom in hospital when I was 5.
Not having Sandy as a friend anymore.

Keep to the ten minute time limit—you might want to set a kitchen timer so you are free to brainstorm your list of losses without being distracted by looking at a clock. At the end of ten minutes continue to the next part of the exercise.

Now claim each loss on your list. Begin by reading each entry aloud to yourself. After reading each one aloud, say: "This is *my* loss; it belongs to me." Then close your eyes and spend a couple of minutes re-living the events surrounding each loss. As you re-live each loss, breathe deeply, loosen your jaw, relax your shoulders, and pay attention to your body. You may find your body suddenly tensing; your eyes may fill with tears or a sob rise in your throat; or you may be aware that you are very uncomfortable. How strongly your body responds to re-living each loss will tell you how important that loss still is to you and that it may be a significant factor contributing to your present depression. Your body is very smart, so trust the signals it sends you.

When you have finished re-living each loss and listened to your body's response, write a few descriptive words about each loss on the right side of your journal page opposite where it is recorded on the left. These descriptive words may include your body's reaction to the re-lived loss or any other thoughts or feelings that surfaced. For example:

Broken engagement with John.	*Began to sob. Very sad. Want him back.*
Mom in hospital when I was 5.	*Not much reaction. I missed her.*
Not having Sandy as a friend anymore.	*Throat tightened. Would love to talk to her again.*

After jotting down a few descriptive words opposite each loss, read over your list again. Are there any losses that feel unresolved? Are there any losses that still cause powerful emotional or physical reactions? If so, those losses may be contributing to your present depression and you need to consciously mourn them.

Close your journal. Take a break before continuing this chapter.

Mourning Your Losses

Once you have named and claimed the losses you have experienced, they must be mourned. Mourning is an outward, external expression of internal grief. Usually mourning is expressed with the help of some kind of ritual, like a funeral or a memorial service.

Mourning rituals have been pretty watered down in twentieth-century America. We tend to sanitize our grief over loss, keeping it locked up inside, and trickle feed our depressions with tiny streams of unresolved grief. Other countries and cultures are much better than we are at helping their people cope with loss and grief so they can get on with their lives. Some time-honored mourning rituals in other cultures include: wakes and wailing; putting on sackcloth and ashes; making solitary pilgrimages to deserts or mountains; painting the mourner's face gray or black; taking a year off from work when a spouse or parent dies. In such cultures mourning rituals are healthy expressions of grief.

A friend of mine told me of a mourning ritual she performed after her fiancé was killed in World War II. Every day she put on a record of sad music. She would sit next to the phonograph and listen to it. She would sob and let the tears roll down her face. She did this for a long time. Then one day she repeated her ritual of playing sad music on the phonograph. She had her tissues handy and was prepared to cry, but that day no tears came. Her flood of grief had been used up. Her body knew better than her conscious mind that she had finished mourning her loss. She was free to continue her life without the depressing burden of unexpressed grief.

Exercise

Open your journal and re-read your list of losses. Choose one loss that continues to have emotional and physical power in your life today. Experiment with mourning your loss and expressing your grief by performing one of the following suggested rituals.

Read over the list of General Mourning Rituals as you would read a menu. If you are divorced, also read the Divorce Rituals list. Not all rituals listed will fit your particular loss, but select one that feels appropriate, one you believe will help you work through any grief you still carry.

General Mourning Rituals

1. Spend an evening, or many evenings, listening to all the sad music you can find.
2. Wear a black armband for two weeks as you work around the house, exercise, or work in the garden.
3. Call a florist and have them send you a white rose every month for a year.
4. Write a poem that describes your loss, expresses any feelings you still have, and says goodbye.
5. Write a letter to the object or subject of your loss, putting as much emotion into the letter as you can.

6. Put a strip of red cloth around or on each place on your body where you have been wounded or scarred.

7. Visit the grave of someone you've lost through death.

8. With high ceremony bury an object in your backyard (or a big flowerpot, if you live in an apartment) that symbolizes your loss—use music, say a eulogy, write and post an epitaph.

9. Go to the ocean or a lake with a weighted bag containing an object that symbolizes whatever loss you need to let go of. Swim out a ways, take a boat, or stand on a dock and throw the bag into the water.

10. Tell a trusted friend, sponsor, or counselor about your loss. Communicate the power of your grief and how it is contributing to your depression. Ask him or her to help you create your own special ritual to mourn your loss.

Divorce Rituals

1. Pour a favorite beverage in a cup or glass. Toast the memories of your marriage and drink the beverage. Put the cup or glass in a sturdy paper bag. Take the bag outside and use a hammer to smash the bag with the glass or cup still inside.

2. Melt down your wedding ring and have it made into something else.

3. Burn your marriage license, then smear your face with the ashes. Wash yourself clean in an ocean, lake, or bathtub.

4. Create a ceremony to honor the memory of your marriage and say goodbye to your spouse. Invite one or two close friends to join you in the ceremony.

These lists are not complete. Feel free to create your own mourning ritual and do it.

Once you have selected an appropriate ritual, perform it, being alert to the voice inside you that says by performing a mourning ritual you are only feeling sorry for yourself. Tell yourself that it is necessary to mourn as a way of moving through your depression and getting on with your life. Be compassionate and kind to the part of you that needs to mourn your loss.

After performing your ritual, open your journal and record your experience. When writing, describe the process of choosing and planning your mourning ritual. Then describe how you performed it. Finally, record your emotional and physical reactions to the ritual: How did it feel emotionally and physically? What sort of effect did performing the ritual have on your depression?

Depression can result from experiencing a small as well as a great loss. As you continue to journal on your journey of recovery, be sure to record any losses you experience and to mourn them. Return to the Mourning Rituals or Divorce Rituals exercise for inspiration or use your own creativity in making rituals to recognize and honor your loss.

Challenging Negative Thinking

A wise man once said that life is 10 percent what happens to you and 90 percent how you respond to what happens to you. In other words, the quality of life is often determined by how well we respond to the daily ups and downs life brings. Sometimes we may slip into focusing on the negative aspects of our lives, especially if we have suffered a series of losses. During such times a depression is often the result, and we find ourselves in a pattern of thinking negatively about our lives. After a while all we see is that the glass is half empty instead of half full. If we allow negative thinking to take hold of our lives, we may become like the mother who gave her son two shirts for his birthday. The son wore one of the shirts to his birthday party. When his mother saw her son in his new shirt, she said to him, "What's wrong? Didn't you like the other shirt?" When negative thinking becomes a pattern, there is just no way to win, and recovery from addiction and depression comes to a grinding halt.

When you are depressed and have slipped into a pattern of negative thinking, you must challenge the tyranny of your thought life. Begin to challenge negative thinking by examining any assumptions you may have about how life should be. Look for the "shoulds" you have about life. For example, you may believe that life should always be fair, or that you should have all of your needs met comfortably and according to schedule. Or you may assume that everybody should like you all of the time. You may secretly believe that God should be responsible for all of your misfortunes, or that you should be responsible for your parent's pain. Finally, you may assume that should you become a different, better person, you wouldn't have such overwhelming problems.

Such assumptions, or "shoulds," about life are often the seeds that sprout negative thoughts. You choose to respond negatively to the daily ups and downs in your life. But it is possible to choose to respond to the hard knocks in life positively. In order to transform negative thought patterns into positive ones that enhance recovery, you must first clear the ground of hidden assumptions. When you are depressed, take an inventory of the "shoulds" that grow into negative thoughts about your life. The following exercise will help you make an inventory of your assumptions and negative thinking so that a positive response to life can take their place.

Exercise

Open your journal. Close your eyes for a moment and recall a recent event that contributed to your depression. Once you have that event in mind, briefly describe the event in your journal.

Record any specific feelings that surfaced as you lived through the event, such as anger, sadness, grief, or frustration. Now play detective for a moment: Try to look for any hidden assumptions or negative thoughts that lay underneath your emotional reaction to that event. Those hidden assumptions and negative thoughts feed your emotional response to an event.

For example, your journal entry with this exercise may look something like this:

Event: Last week I didn't get that promotion I deserved.

Emotions: Anger, frustration, self-hate, hopelessness.

Assumptions/negative thinking: Life should be fair—I deserved that promotion. I should always be rewarded for good work. If life isn't fair, what's the point of hoping for anything anymore? Everybody at work should like me and show it—since I didn't get the promotion, it must mean nobody likes me.

Spend at least fifteen minutes looking for the hidden "shoulds" and negative thoughts underneath your emotional reaction to the event and record them in your journal.

Now spend another fifteen minutes transforming the negative thought patterns you've uncovered into positive responses. For example, underneath your list of hidden assumptions and negative thinking, you may add something like this:

Positive thoughts/responses: So, life isn't fair after all. That means I must take care of myself. I'm going to consider having a positive, constructive talk with my boss about the situation. Not getting the promotion does not mean I am a bad person or that everybody hates me. It just means that rewards for good work are not automatic. I know I am doing the best I can at my job. I don't have to beat myself up because I didn't get promoted. I am proud of my work.

Once you have recorded your positive thoughts and responses, re-read what you have written there. Let the positive thoughts and responses sink deep inside you. As you continue through the week, return to the positive thoughts and responses, and re-read them. Take those thoughts out of your journal and into your life.

Cultivating positive thoughts and responses to events that depress you will be of great help in recovering from depression. When life gives you a hard knock, return to this exercise, take an inventory of hidden "shoulds" and negative thoughts, and frame a positive way of looking at the situation.

Re-directing Anger

Most depression is anger turned inside and directed at ourselves. In recovering from depression we must learn to re-direct that anger in a healthy way.

Negative thoughts and feelings about ourselves often fuel anger. Such negativity about ourselves only deepens our agony. We weren't born with such negativity and anger—we absorbed it during our childhood and youth. We learned not to hurt others with our anger, so we turn the anger inside and use it against ourselves.

Think for a moment about your life right now and about how you usually handle anger. It may be easier for you to make yourself the target of your anger rather than someone you love. After all, you reason, you can't get angry with your family—you may hurt them. So out of protective loyalty to loved ones, you get mad at yourself instead of one of them.

The following exercise helps you to identify how you learned anger from your family of origin. Once you have identified that, you'll have the freedom to re-direct your anger in appropriate healthy ways that enhance your recovery.

Exercise

Open your journal. Draw a line down the center of the page. Now close your eyes for a moment. Recall three times (one time from adolescence; one time from childhood; and one time from early childhood) when you or one of your family members got really angry. Briefly jot down on the left side of the journal page your age at the time, the event associated with the anger, and your memory of how you felt in the situation. As you remember and record each memory, pay special attention to how your body responds to the memory. For example, your entry may look something like this:

Age 18; I wrecked the car.
Terrified of Dad's response.
Now I hold my breath.

Age 9; Dad passed out in living
room before the party.
Scared by Mom's 3-day silence.
Remembering now makes me
shiver.

Age 5; Mom yelling at Jim.
Thought it was my fault.

It does not matter whether the anger was directed at you or another family member. What is important is that you identify your response to the anger that surrounded you.

On the right side of the page, record how your family expressed anger in reaction to the event. For example:

Age 18; I wrecked the car.   *Dad threatened to hit me but*
Terrified of Dad's response.   *Mom intervened.*
Now I hold my breath.

Once you have recorded how your family handled anger, go back and re-read what you have written. As you reflect on how your family expressed anger, you may wish to ask yourself the following questions:

Was anger acknowledged directly?
In the incidents you have described, was anger avoided or ignored?
Was the anger resolved or did it linger for a long time?
Was forgiveness ever asked or offered?
Were your parents the only ones allowed to be angry?

You may want to continue writing in your journal answering one or more of these questions. You could also choose to spend some time writing about your body's present reactions to memories of anger. Such physical reactions may be clues that you are still carrying anger you absorbed from your family of origin.

Every family has its own anger "coat of arms." This coat of arms, unique to each family, represents how a family fights. Each family teaches its young to fight by word and deed. If there's a difference between the walk and the talk, children will learn the walk.

Somewhere along the way you have learned to turn your weapon, whatever it might be, on yourself. You specialize in unconsciously shooting yourself in the foot because you don't "deserve" success; you tend to jump on live landmines to protect others' feelings; you're prone toward making tiny little razor cuts on your psyche to punish yourself. Such self-destructive skills are a learned art form that bears some thinking, feeling, and journaling.

A family's armory is varied. Sometimes anger comes out as a set of tiny critical knives that whittle away at the other's ankles (or your own). Other times family members specialize in sniper fire from hidden, unexpected ambush sites. Some may use poison gases of criticism that leave you short of breath. Some family gladiators like the ball and net; they become expert in tripping you up in a guilt mesh.

One past student of mine was so cold that she, like a titanic iceberg, created her own weather around her; most of her family had either been lost in her fog, sunk in her icy waters, or frozen for years. I also knew a dad who had learned how to suck all the oxygen out of the room with his empty-feeling world and inability to attach to anyone; his children still gasp for a breath of feeling when in his presence.

With some families what you don't see is what you get. One person's loss is another's gain. The mother or father, for example, may participate in this family swap meet by absenting themselves of all mad feelings with a smile or comment. These angry, unclaimed feelings get picked up by the person in the family who is the most sensitive. This person senses the anger, sucks it in (by taking responsibility for the unclaimed emotion), and gradually gets loaded down with this unclaimed feeling. Much of the time we call this depression.

Exercise

Think about your own family's armor. Begin by describing the fight style of those family members on the periphery and then move toward the core. Begin with your extended family (that is, grandparents, significant aunts and uncles, and cousins). Then move to your immediate family of origin (parents, siblings, parent figures). Next describe your current nuclear family. Finally describe your own personal fight style.

Realize that your style in the office may well be different from your style at home, with your friends, or when you go to visit your folks. You might want to write in your journal about how your fight style has changed over the years. On the other hand, you might do better to draw pictures of your self fighting as a child, as an adolescent, and at various phases in your adult life. Finally you might want to make a few different symbols (in clay, computer graphics, tapestry, weaving, crayon, or other forms you might be comfortable attempting) to show how your own fight style has changed.

The point of this exercise is to learn to honor the emerging warrior or warrioress who is struggling to channel anger in the service of life instead of death. Journaled anger allows you to expand your choices and use greater consciousness in your personal weaponry and style. Our inner truth surfaces and then it sets us free.

Now that you have identified ways in which you absorbed some of the anger in your family of origin, experiment in your journal with constructive ways to re-direct that anger. The following are suggestions for using your journal to stop turning anger on your self and channel it outward in healthy ways.

When you have uncovered unresolved anger toward someone, or should you discover a lot of negative, angry thoughts about your self, use your journal as a safe place to begin to get the anger outside of your self. Using your journal in this way helps you recover from depression. You have already experimented with some of the techniques suggested below in other exercises in this book. Return to this Suggestions for Journaling section whenever you feel ready to explore and re-direct your anger.

Suggestions for Journaling

Use one or more of the following journaling techniques in exploring and re-directing your anger to recover from depression.

Exercise

Write a letter in your journal to the person at whom you are angry. You will never send this letter through the mail—it is only a way to get some of the anger outside your self and on to the page. This is a very useful technique if the person at whom you are angry is either dead or separated by time and distance. Writing a letter is helpful if you are unwilling to express your anger to the person directly. When writing such a letter, express your anger. Record feelings, not just thoughts. When you are finished, sign and date your letter.

Exercise

Place an empty chair in front of you. Imagine the person you are angry at is sitting in front of you. Open your journal and create a dialogue between you and the person you have imagined in the empty chair. In other words, have a good, old-fashioned argument in your journal. Write until you and the person in the chair have nothing more to say to each other right now. You may resolve your argument and anger, or you may return to the argument later and continue the dialogue.

Exercise

Assemble some crayons, colored pencils, or felt tip pens. Open your journal and draw what your anger feels like to you. You don't have to draw a picture or an image—you may just want to put colors on the paper. At first nothing may come or you may not feel very angry. Keep drawing until you fill as much of the page as you can.

After completing the drawing, write a brief description of your experience in your journal. This technique is especially useful when you think your depression may be the result of anger, but you are not sure. It is a good way to explore what feelings may or may not be there.

Exercise

Write a prayer to God. Tell God how angry you are and at whom you are angry. It is okay to be angry at God in your prayer. Be as honest as you can about how you feel. Close the prayer by asking God for healing and resolution to your anger.

Exercise

Select a container from your house or garden in which you can put your anger. Put the container in front of you. Imagine filling the container with your anger—feel the anger leaving your body and flowing into the container.

Now open your journal and describe the container in detail: What color is it? Is it large or small? What kind of shape does it have? Next describe how it holds your anger. You may want to use some of the following questions to get you started: Does the object leak? Is it about to explode or break? Is it full or half-empty? When filled with your anger, is it heavy or light-weight? Is your anger spilling over the top?

Put down your pen and lay your journal aside for a moment. Taking the container with you, find an appropriate place to pour out your anger. It may be the backyard, the garbage can, down the drain in the tub or sink, or you may decide to put it in another container. Pour out your anger in the place you have selected.

Finally, pick up your pen and journal again. Briefly record where you poured out your anger and why you selected that particular place as a receptacle for your anger.

Summary

In this chapter you've learned that depression is a natural part of the recovery journey. You have also learned how to recover from depression. You now have a variety of ways in which to experience hope as you mourn your losses, challenge negative thinking, and channel your anger.

Continue by reading the next chapter, "The Dream Journal," or select another chapter in which to explore your recovery.

The

Dream

Journal

Dreams and Recovery

In the Bible we read of prophets, kings, priests, and apostles who routinely explored their dreams for important messages about how to conduct their lives. Not only did the Lord appear in dreams to his people throughout biblical history, God also speaks to us through our dreams. And he uses our dreams to further our journeys in recovery.

Bethyl and I have been keeping dream journals for thirty-five years, and they have revealed priceless information for our recovery. Through dreams God has given both of us warnings, encouragement, and clues about what to do with our lives. Dreams allow us to get in touch with those deeper, wiser parts of our selves that are our companions on our journeys toward healing.

Countless mental health professionals, pastors, and ministers believe in the power of dreams to instruct, confront, comfort, and challenge. It is possible for you to interpret and understand your dreams, and it is a very practical process. Your dreams help you answer such practical questions as: What do I need to recover on my own recovery journey? Where do I need to go from here? Am I on the right track? How can I experience deeper healing? This chapter distills the basic theory and practice of recording, interpreting, and understanding your dreams to aid your recovery.

How to Recover and Record Dreams

Shakespeare once wrote that sleeping and dreaming are "nature's chief feast."[1] But many of us never enjoy the banquet table of our dreams because upon awakening we forget them. We spend a third of our lives sleeping and dreaming and, when we do not remember and recover our dreams, a third of life's valuable, healing lessons pass unnoticed. You may be saying, "But I never remember my dreams!" That doesn't have to remain true. You can remember, record, enjoy, and learn from your dreams. If you practice the following suggestions, in no time you will be recovering your dreams.

Getting Started

You may want to keep a separate dream journal in which you only record and work with your dreams. Or you may use your regular, daily journal to record your dreams alongside your other entries. The value of a separate dream journal is that you can always keep it next to your bed. Should you choose to work with your dreams in your daily journal, you must remember to bring it to bed with you each night. Use a journal that is most convenient for you now.

Keep a small, slender flashlight, fastened to a pen with rubber bands, beside your bed. This will enable you to write in your dream journal during the night without turning on a light, searching for a pen, and waking your spouse.

Beginning to recover your dreams is a five step process that roughly outlines the process of recording and living your dreams. This chapter will explain each of these steps more fully as you read and work the exercises. But first, copy these five steps in the front of your dream journal for handy reference:

 1. *Remember the dream or fragments of it.*

 2. *Immediately record what you remember.*

 3. *Ask yourself a few crucial questions about the dream.*

4. Choose one part of the dream to write about in your journal.

5. Make this dream a part of your external recovery program.

Before you go to bed at night, open your dream journal and write the date at the top of the left-hand page. Record your dream on this left-hand page, leaving the right-hand page blank for working with the dream at a later time.

Remembering

Now you are ready to begin. Before going to sleep at night, tell yourself, "I want to remember what I dream!" Repeat this to yourself a few times before falling asleep and ask God to teach you in the night. Be like young Samuel in 1 Samuel 3:3–11 and listen when God calls your name in the night.

Should you wake up in the middle of the night, either to go to the bathroom or because a dream actually awakens you, jot down in your dream journal exactly what is in your head as you wake up. When you get up in the morning, before getting out of bed, again jot down whatever is on your mind as you wake up. This process will help you remember your dreams. On first awakening, you may be able to remember only a fragment of a dream or a series of disconnected images. That is just fine. Make a commitment to yourself to jot down whatever you remember no matter how fleeting or how strange.

Often you will find your dreams are quite pleasant. But occasionally they may be confusing, or they may be frightening nightmares. During such times you may be tempted to forget them or want to change the memories of the dreams. Resist this temptation and record whatever you can.

When writing in the middle of the night or first thing in the morning, don't worry about neatness or complete sentences, and don't spend a lot of time writing. Literally jot down whatever you wake up with. Later you will return to your dream journal and work on the dream. When describing your dream, use the first person, present tense. For example:

I'm running to class.
I have a final exam.
I haven't read the books. I panic.

Writing in the first person and in the present tense will help you re-live the experience of the dream later when you return to work more intensely with it.

Give yourself permission to forget dreams on some mornings. Dreams are elusive creatures. If you put too much pressure on your self to remember, performance anxiety will chase the dreams away. As always, be patient and loving with yourself. Remember, recovering your dreams is fun!

If you practice these suggestions and still find it difficult to remember your dreams, don't be discouraged. Try waking your self with an alarm clock after about four and a half hours of sleep. This might help you capture your dream as it's happening.

Should you continue to forget your dreams each night, write a dialogue in your journal with the part of you who resists remembering your dreams. Such a dialogue might look like this:

I WANT TO HEAR WHAT MY   *i don't want you to remember.*
DREAM IS SAYING TO ME
TONIGHT!

WHY NOT?   *you may change.*

WHAT'S WRONG WITH THAT?   *i'm frightened of change. let me*
                                      tell you about some of my
                                      fears . . .

Writing a dialogue with the part of you who resists remembering your dreams often will remove the barrier to your dream world, and remembering your dreams will be easier.

If your spouse is also keeping a dream journal, promise each other that neither of you will read the other's journal without permission.

Honor your boundaries in this way. Each of you must have the freedom either to share a dream with the other or to keep it private.

Sharing

Sometimes you may choose to share a dream with your spouse or a close, trusted friend. When reading from your dream journal with someone you trust, read the entry aloud the way you wrote it (in the first person, present tense) as though the dream is happening as you read. It is best that your friend or spouse not interpret the dream for you. Rather he or she should ask you these questions: What are your associations with the dream? Where is your attention drawn to in the dream? What are your feelings about the dream?

Once you have answered these questions, you can invite another's thoughts and feelings about your dream, but never before you've offered your own interpretation.

After you have begun to remember and record your dreams, return to your dream journal to begin interpreting their meaning.

How to Interpret Your Dreams

Dreams tell us important things about our lives and our recovery, such as how we experience our inner conflicts and addictive impulses. Dreams show us how we relate to the many part-selves of our family of self. They also tell us how we experience the world in general and significant others in our personal worlds in particular. In other words, dreams hold important information we can use in recovery. Recovery includes identifying inner conflicts and addictive impulses, learning to take better care of our inner selves, and developing healthy relationships with the world, as well as with those we love. Interpreting our dreams creates a map for our recovery journeys, for dreams offer us direction on our journeys toward healing.

Interpreting your dreams is a process of learning to ask the right questions of each dream. The images and symbols that make up dreams should not be taken as literal fact. The language of dreams involves symbols and imagination. Once you have jotted a dream in your journal, you must return to it when you are fully awake and have time to interpret its meaning. Each dream has a message just for you. Asking your dream the right questions is the key that unlocks the message.

Below is a list of twelve important questions to ask each dream. Answering these questions will help you interpret the message. Read through the list and then complete the exercise.

1. What is the theme of my dream? What title can I give this dream to best represent its theme?

2. What is happening in my life *right now* that might have triggered this dream? Why did I have this dream last night instead of last month or a year ago?

3. What symbol in the dream attracts me most? (It could be a person, place, thing, or activity.) What feelings do I experience around this symbol—am I mad, sad, glad, scared?

4. How close or far away am I in the dream? Am I watching the dream the way I watch a movie, or am I playing a central role in the drama of the dream? Do I become more passive or active as the dream progresses?

5. Who or what in the dream feels dangerous? (In dream symbols the enemy will often become your best friend if you treat him or her with respect. If you ignore or disrespect the frightening symbol, it will become more threatening in other dreams as time goes on.)

6. Is anything or anyone being harmed in my dream? How do I feel toward the person, thing, or creature that is being hurt or wounded? Does this person, thing, or creature correspond to a part of me, or someone close to me, who is hurting?

7. Is there any sexual activity in my dream? If so, what does this sexual activity mean? (When sexual activity appears in a dream, people in recovery are often tempted to block the

image or feel ashamed of it. Sexual activity in dreams usually is a symbol for a merger or a coming together of forbidden parts of your self. In other words, healing and integration in your family of self is occurring. So be curious about sexual symbols in your dreams and explore their meaning for you. And remember that the appearance of sexual activity in a dream does not mean that in real life you really want to have sex with the person in your dream.)

8. What or who is being aggressive in my dream? Is one person in the dream angry with another? (Aggression in a dream often means you are hostile toward another part of your self, or that a part of your self is hostile toward your conscious self.)

9. What or who am I avoiding in this dream? How am I being evasive? What part of this dream did I enjoy the most? In what ways was it pleasant or comforting?

10. Who or what is being wounded in this dream? How is this like a part of me that is hurting in some way?

11. Who am I in this dream? What is my identity or name? How do I behave and feel? Is my sense of my identity in the dream strong or weak?

12. What is my dream wanting, demanding, or asking in response from me right now? What specific action can I take in my real, outer life to show the dream that I have heard its message?

Exercise

Select a dream from your dream journal and ask the questions listed above. Not all twelve questions will be appropriate for every dream, but use as many of them as you can. On the right-hand page, opposite the record of your dream, write the answers to the questions.

The following is an example from my dream journal:

Roasting

It's midnight. I am in a deep jungle in the heart of Africa. I'm watching a group of warriors dancing in a torch-lit circle around a huge bonfire. Drums are beating. On the fire four deer are being roasted in a sacrificial ritual. The second deer from the left, a doe, raises her head and tastes her own breast meat, next to her heart, to see whether she is finished cooking. After a while she puts her head back down and submits to more roasting. She knows she isn't done.

Questions and Answers

What's the theme? Tolerating suffering without running away from pain.

What symbol attracts me most? The sacrificial deer.

What feelings go with this symbol? Terror and astonishment that the doe tolerates the heat of her heart's pain at midnight.

Am I an active or passive participant? I become increasingly close to the central action piece, the deer, as the dream progresses, but I am still a spectator rather than an active participant.

What is my identity in this dream? I alternate between being behind the camera, watching the dream, and being the deer. I can stand the deer's suffering only so long. Then I move back behind the camera.

What is the dream asking me to do? I'm being asked to honor the suffering in my heart. Some action in my outer life is being asked of me also—I must worship God so that I can be still and steady in my suffering.

When you have answered as many of the questions as you can, close your dream journal until later.

Further Suggestions for Interpreting Dreams

You have experimented with interpreting a dream, understood its basic theme, given the dream a title, and answered a few of the questions to understand the dream's message. What follows are other techniques to help you further explore your dreams and unlock their messages for you.

Re-learning Lessons from Dreams by Making Associations

Often dream images are concrete reminders of some essential lessons in your life that you once learned but have since forgotten to apply. Once you've completed the task of asking and answering questions, look again at your dream. What associations do you make between the inner world of the dream and the outer world of real life? Is there a lesson that you may have learned long ago, but have forgotten? If so, how does the lesson you learn from your dream impact your present recovery?

These are a few associations I made in my *Roasting* dream:

I associate the flames of the fire with the suffering in my life. I associate the darkness with recent losses I would rather avoid feeling, even though I know it is healthy to express grief over loss. I associate the doe as a Christ symbol, who teaches me about patience in suffering.

Writing a few associations like this will help you recover old lessons you may have already learned in recovery. You can apply them to new challenges you have now.

Merging with Dream Images

In order to really understand another person, as the old saying goes, walk a mile in his shoes. This practice is useful when you are working with images and symbols from your dreams. You really begin to experience the power of a dream image when, by using your imagination, you merge with the image.

Exercise

Choose the image or symbol from your dream that feels the most exciting, intriguing, fearful, or energizing. Then close your eyes and imagine the image. Become the image or symbol. Try to feel it from the inside out. Using all of your senses, smell, taste, hear, see, and feel in your own body what it is like to be the image from your dream. Then open your eyes and your dream journal. Write in the first person, present tense, as though you are the dream image.

I had a dream about Nazis during World War II looting an old house as they looked for Jews. I decided to merge with the image of the secret trapdoor in the house. This is what I recorded in my dream journal about merging with the trapdoor:

I'm the creaky, wooden trapdoor that hides the Jewish children from the Gestapo who are now ransacking the house. I'm sturdy with metal hinges on the bottom side. I am solid without betraying feelings. I fit flush with the rest of the floorboards. No one knows the treasure I am hiding underneath me.

Often the symbol or image you choose to merge with represents a semi-conscious part of you that can give you important information about your recovery. Many times merging with dream images shows you where to grow in recovery. The process of merging with a symbol in your dream allows the symbol to communicate with you on the page in your journal.

Writing a Dialogue with Dream Symbols

Approach all dream symbols or images as various members of your family of self, remembering that these various parts of you live in your unconscious or semi-conscious mind. Even though you're not consciously aware of all of them, the members of your family of self have much to communicate to you about your recovery journey. To communicate with your family of self, use your dream journal to write dialogues with them. Writing dialogues with dream images involves the same technique outlined in Chapter 1. You may want to review that earlier section of the book.

Exercise

Choose a symbol or image from a dream. On the right-hand page of your dream journal, opposite the dream you've recorded, begin a dialogue with the image. Start by closing your eyes and imagining the figure from your dream. Then ask the image questions such as: Who are you? Why are you coming to me in my dream now? What do you want to say to me? What kind of action do you require from me? Listen very carefully for the dream image's response. As the symbol begins to respond, write the answers in your dream journal. Go back and forth, questioning and answering until you feel the dialogue is complete.

You may want to dialogue with several images or symbols from a dream. Or you may want to arrange a dialogue between dream symbols. For example, after I merged with the wooden trapdoor in the dream I described above, I could have created a dialogue between the trapdoor and the Jewish children hiding below.

It is also possible to write dialogues with feelings, memories, or tiny fragments of a dream. Some mornings you will awaken with hardly a trace of a dream, but you will find a memory coming to you or an emotion brooding in you. Create a dialogue in your dream journal with that memory or feeling. Often I awaken in the morning to a song playing in my head, but no real memory of a dream. On those mornings I write a dialogue with the song, treating it as a dream image, asking it questions, and listening for answers. Whatever feeling, memory, or image you wake with in the morning is a gift that may offer insight to your recovery. Communicate with it by writing a dialogue.

Re-working a Dream

Many times you wake to find you have not finished your dream, and you are left with feelings of incompleteness. Or sometimes a dream refuses to communicate with you. No matter how many critical questions you ask it or how many dialogues you write, the dream refuses to yield its treasure at this time.

When you experience an unfinished dream or a dream that is difficult to understand, you can try to re-work it. The re-working technique involves returning to the dream and either creating an ending for it or inserting another element into its main portion. In other words, you won't try simply to explore the cast of characters in your dream drama, but you will become the writer and director of your dream as well. Since the technique of re-working a dream uses your imagination, you will find the relaxation exercise from Chapter 1 very helpful. Use it before re-working a dream so your imagination can be fully involved.

Exercise

When you are relaxed and ready, look at the unfinished dream. Return to the page in your dream journal where you have recorded as much of the dream as possible. Re-read the dream until it comes alive in your imagination. Close your eyes and see the dream unfold. Then free your imagination to finish the dream. Try asking yourself: How would I like this dream to end? What sort of ending would feel most natural? Once you have imagined an ending for the dream, open your eyes and record the ending in your dream journal.

Exercise

Now work with a difficult dream. Re-read the record of the dream in your journal. Read until it comes alive in your imagination. Close your eyes and return to the place in this dream that is most puzzling or confusing. Ask yourself: What person, thing, place, or activity does this part of my dream need in order for me to understand what the dream is trying to say to me? When an answer presents itself, insert that person, thing, place, or activity into the dream. Let your imagination run free with this new element in your dream. Imagine how the dream would play itself out with the new element. Then open your eyes and either record your experience with the new element in your dream, or re-write the dream as it unfolded anew in your imagination.

Once you have re-worked your dream, either adding an ending or an insert to the dream, you may continue to work with the dream by making associations, merging with images, or writing a dialogue with parts of the dream.

A note of caution is needed here. Sometimes dreams are incomplete or deeply puzzling because they contain frightening material. If as you re-work your dream you find it too frightening, you can choose how to proceed. You can set the dream aside and not work with it until later, or you can ask God to walk with you through it. As you re-play the dream in your imagination, imagine also that God is walking with you in it. Or you can share the dream with a trusted loved one or a therapist who can offer support and guidance as you work with a frightening dream.

Re-working a dream is a very creative, imaginative process. It can be a great deal of fun. Approach your dreams like a child and always explore them with a deep sense of curiosity and playfulness.

Making Your Dreams Come True

Recovering and interpreting your dreams will give you insight important to your recovery. But insight and personal awareness are not enough. You must do something with the information your dreams give you. When insight is married to action, you make your dreams come true, and putting insight into action will have a significant impact on your recovery, on how you care for yourself, and on how you develop healthy relationships with significant individuals in your life and the world in general.

Acting on your dreams also helps keep your dream life active. If you allow your dreams to be merely interesting without acting on what you learn, they will become less frequent and finally dry up altogether. We remember our dreams only when they are important enough for us to integrate them into our waking lives. It's like the parable of the talents in Scripture—if you use your talents, more will be given to you; if you hide what you have, it will be taken away.

These two suggestions will help you make your dreams come true in your waking life. These are only suggestions to get you started. As you experiment with these, you will eventually want to create your own ways of bringing your dreams into your life and recovery. There are no rules for making your dreams a part of reality. Be as creative as your imagination allows.

Using Visual and Musical Arts

Some dreams will want to move beyond words and take some kind of artistic shape. Experiment with making your dream come true by using various art materials to describe it or put it to music. It is a good idea to store some general art supplies somewhere in your home: a large, over-sized pad of drawing paper; crayons; colored pencils; felt tip pens; water-based paints and brushes; and perhaps even some modeling clay. If you play a musical instrument, make sure one is handy.

When you have a dream you feel deserves artistic interpretation, make that a reality through art or music. If you choose to make your dream more real through art, decide which medium to work with. Then either draw or represent the main scene or symbol from your dream that most captures your imagination.

Sometimes music may seem like a better way to honor your dream. A number of years ago Bethyl dreamed of walking up to an old abandoned barn that was shut tight. It seemed like no one had visited there for years. With some effort, she pushed open a creaky, rusted door. Inside the barn two brightly colored parakeets sang cheerily and flew down from the rafters to greet her. Bethyl was amazed that anything living could have survived so long in that abandoned place.

After recording the dream in her dream journal, Bethyl connected the dream to parakeets she had as a child. She decided the best way to act on her dream was to play and sing songs on the piano. Singing was a way of honoring the songs that were still inside her but were abandoned long ago.

Bringing a dream into reality through art work or music helps deepen the experience, feelings, and meaning of the dream. It also helps you make visible any lessons you need to learn from it and apply in your recovery.

Constructing a Dream Task

A dream task, another way of bringing a dream into reality, is either a ritual or an activity that makes the dream's lesson real. For example, if your dream reveals you have not grieved a significant loss, the Mourning Rituals listed in Chapter 2 may be performed as dream tasks.

I had a dream that required me to perform a dream task. In this dream a traffic cop caught me speeding. I argued with him, telling him it was a marginal offense. I said that he ought to be out chasing real criminals! He agreed to give me a task instead of a ticket. The task was to write a big outdoor map. I felt like a kid doing "write offs" after school on a blackboard. While I was writing on the map, huge, lazy iguanas began leaving droppings all over it. I had to keep moving the droppings off my writing. Meanwhile, the policeman leaned against the wall and smiled.

I began to think of a task I could do to bring this dream into reality. I decided to heed the warning from the traffic cop and the lazy iguanas to slow down. Usually I run with my dogs in the hills several times a week, but after I had the dream, I decided to walk the dogs instead of running them. I focused on walking slowly, breathing deeply, and enjoying the trees, grass, and clouds. As I walked, I kept repeating to myself, "Slow down, Vance, slow down. You feel your emotions only when you slow down."

Performing a dream task may be anything as simple as taking a walk, or saying a special prayer in church for the part of you a dream has told you needs healing, or telling the dream to a friend. Dream tasks do not need to be complicated or take a lot of time. The purpose of dream tasks is to help you integrate dream messages into your life and recovery.

Summary

In this chapter you've learned techniques to help you remember, record, and interpret your dreams. You have also learned to make your dreams come true by integrating them into your life and recovery. Recovering your dream life will greatly enhance your recovery journey if you persist with patience and prayer.

5

Journaling

for

Men

Recovery from addiction consists of getting in touch with our feelings, learning to express those feelings in appropriate ways, and building healthy relationships with significant others. It also involves recovering an emotional life that isn't medicated by an addictive substance or relationship.

Much healing in recovery comes from listening to, respecting, and loving the deepest parts of ourselves, but for most men that is very difficult. We simply haven't learned to listen to the calls and conflicts of our inner, emotional lives.

A study done sometime ago revealed that this is due in part to gender differences. Four- and five-year-old girls and boys were studied as they played alone. The girls played make believe, having conversations with imaginary friends, hosting tea parties for stuffed animals, and so forth. As they played, the girls constantly used words to describe their feelings. The boys, on the other hand, made lots of noise, but they used very few words to express what they were feeling. They made sounds of yelping, snorting, and grunting, and were much more physical in their play.

This study underscores what we've known for a long time about the differences between men and women. Women are more inclined to listen to the calls and conflicts of their inner, emotional lives, and they are far more able to express what they hear and feel. Women are more able to relate to each other and to give one another support and encouragement during recovery. Men generally surpass women in mastering and manipulating the outer world of work, economic achievement, and play or sports. While men have friendships with other men and inter-relate, most tend to suppress their personal feelings and needs and focus primarily on their achievements that are apparent to others. Their inner selves remain secret even to themselves.

A vivid example of these differences is what we could expect if we put a group of men and a group of women in different rooms with Cokes and cookies. After twenty minutes, the women would be chatting comfortably among themselves, but in the other room the Cokes, the cookies, and the men would all be gone. The men would have set about the task of eating and, as soon as the cookies and Cokes disappeared, they would go their separate, lonely ways.

Men's inability to be attuned to and express their inner feelings and needs and to understand the complex, invisible webs of human relationships makes journaling a recovery task that proves difficult. The more difficult it seems to be, however, the more necessary and helpful it will be ultimately for building relationships, getting in touch with feelings, and learning to express those feelings in appropriate ways. In short, men in recovery need to journal in order to recover their bodies, souls, and spirits, and to find the words to express the experience of being in recovery.

Recovering Body, Soul, and Spirit

What does it mean to really be a man? For me it means having full access to my body, to my soul and its emotional world, and to my spiritual world. Recovery is a journey toward healing, wholeness, and integration of body, soul, and spirit.

Living Well in My Body

Important parts of my body are my eyes, for I look at the world through them, not through someone else's. But most men from early childhood until about mid-life tend to view the world through someone else's eyes. For example, the things our mothers have said over the years about our fathers have a huge impact on how we view our dads. Therefore, most of us look at our fathers through our mothers' eyes. Not until later in our lives, around mid-life, do we begin to reclaim our own eyes and develop our own vision of our dads as men.

Once we are able to see the world through our own eyes, we can borrow the eyes and the perspectives of others in healthy ways. It's been amazing to me to realize that others' views of the world are totally different from mine. That is why seeing ourselves through the eyes of someone we trust is critical to our recovery. Feedback from someone else, such as a sponsor, is immensely helpful in charting our recovery journeys.

Other important parts of my body are my feet. Like most men, I must anchor that part of me who flees commitment in relationships. Being aware of my feet touching the ground helps remind me that I don't always have to live in my head. I can live lower down to the ground as well. In recovery I need to keep my feet on the ground.

My good friend, Hank, and I had a deep and lasting friendship that began in the late sixties. We were tennis partners; we traveled through Europe and the Middle East together; we smuggled Bibles behind the Iron Curtain; we were scuba diving buddies; and, as professional therapists, we worked together.

In the summer of 1979, we were on one of our scuba diving adventures, and while we were on the ocean floor, 110 feet below the surface, Hank died. I panicked and felt crazy for a while. Death had come very close and almost claimed me along with Hank. I began to run away from life, and eventually I became addicted to running as fast as I could go. I took up flying small airplanes. I rode motorcycles too fast. I ran faster and faster to avoid committed relationships with either men or women.

After several years of working through my fear of getting close to another man, I developed a close friendship with another buddy, Earl. In many ways our friendship parallels the one I had with Hank. Now Earl and I look back on a decade of playing, talking seriously, and being accountable to each other as good friends. Still, even today, it is easy for me to indulge my addiction to moving fast and flying away from important relationships like the one I have with Earl. But my feet keep me on the ground and working my recovery by taking one step at a time.

My feet also help me set appropriate, healthy boundaries. Those of us in recovery know how important appropriate boundaries are, for good boundaries help define who we are. They are the basis for forming healthy, addiction-free relationships. As a man, I must know who to let inside my boundaries and who to keep out. A man who stays on his feet is able to walk the ramparts of the castle of his self and patrol the borders of his kingdom. Such a man has a healthy view of his limits, as well as his potential.

Exercise

Set aside thirty minutes for taking a walk. You may want to just walk around the neighborhood, or you could go to a park to walk. Be sure to take a wrist watch with you, for this exercise requires that you time yourself in completing different parts of the exercise.

Before you begin walking, note the time. Spend the first ten minutes feeling your feet move across the pavement, dirt, or grass. Concentrate on your feet. Look down at them as you walk. While you are watching your feet and concentrating on them, ask yourself the following questions: What does walking feel like? Do your feet pound the pavement or touch it lightly? Do your feet move briskly or do they stroll? Is walking pleasurable or is it simply another task? After you've thought about the answers to these questions, spend the remainder of the ten minutes feeling the ground under your feet as you walk. When the ten minutes are up, you may stop watching your feet.

Spend the next ten minutes walking as slowly as you can. Take two or three deep breaths, look at the scenery, and go slowly. As you walk, ask yourself: Where are my feet taking me on my recovery journey? Where am I going in recovery? How am I enjoying myself on this journey? Continue to walk slowly until another ten minutes have gone by.

Spend the remaining ten minutes enjoying the walk you are taking. *Try not to think anything at all.* Just be aware of your body enjoying a walk. You may walk slowly or quickly. The important thing now is to walk in whatever way gives you the most pleasure.

At the end of thirty minutes return to your journal. Open it and record your walking experience. Write about how you concentrated on the movement of your feet, and what you noticed about them. Next write about walking slowly. Was it difficult or easy and why? Then spend some time writing about where your feet are taking you in recovery. Are you getting there quickly or slowly? Are you enjoying the journey? Finally, write generally about your experience of taking this walk. What did you like about it? What was difficult?

You may return to this exercise again and again as a way of checking in with your self about where you are in your recovery. Too often we men get caught up in the goal of recovery, which is to "get there," and we deny ourselves the joy of the journey itself. When you feel frustrated with not accomplishing enough in your recovery, take this walk again.

Another important part of claiming my body is owning my male sexuality. The word *genitals* came originally from a word that means "beginnings," but it also means "initiative." Being in touch with your male sexuality means having the ability to take healthy social initiative, as well as sexual initiative. As a man I must be able to take initiative during times of adversity, such as when I've been fired, rejected by a lover, or am coping with significant loss. Taking action is crucial to masculinity.

One of the most important parts of my body is my heart. All too often we men perform heart by-pass surgery on ourselves by ignoring our own feelings. We prefer to live in a heady world of ideas and abstractions, rather than in the unfamiliar world of emotions. Successful recovery means we must recover our feelings and share them in appropriate ways with those we love.

Earlier in this book we looked at the importance of paying attention to our bodies' responses to various exercises and emotional responses. Because your responses are so important, it is crucial for you to record in your journal any physical sensations you have in response to feelings, relationships, or dreams. Journaling about your body will help you recover your body and the joy of being a clean and sober man.

Living Well in My Soul

Living well in your soul means discovering your inner world, the house that holds your emotional life. This fairy tale is about the journey you must make as a recovering man to reclaim your soul.

Everyman and the Hag of Death

Once upon a time, Everyman set out on a journey to recover his soul. Eventually his path led him to a mountain. To continue his journey, Everyman had to climb the mountain and travel past the cave of the Hag of Death. Though Everyman was frightened by the Hag, he summoned all his courage and began to climb.

The Hag of Death saw Everyman toiling up the mountain while he was still a long way off, and she picked up a stick and sketched an intricate design in the dirt. Soon, as Everyman came to the cave, she quickly erased half of her sketch. Then the Hag said to Everyman, "This sketch is you. If you can accurately complete it, I will allow you to continue your journey. And I will direct your way—either up the Mountains of Outer Accomplishments or down into the Underground Caves of Inner Fulfillment. But if you are unable to complete my little picture of you here in the dirt, I will strike you dead where you stand."

In the middle of his journey, in the middle of his life, Everyman looked the Hag of Death in the eye, picked up the stick, and began to complete the picture of himself.

Each one of us must complete a picture of ourselves, for if we don't we can't recover our souls and become whole. The mountains and caves the Hag mentions are different regions in the terrain of our lives, but most of us are accustomed to exploring only the Mountains of Outer Accomplishments. The movement of life from boyhood to manhood is outward and upward. Families, schools, and churches generally encourage us to achieve, initiate, and take action, and we tend to view our lives as successful if, as the old hymn, "Higher Ground," says, we are "pressing on the upward way," gaining "new heights every day."

True masculine development does involve climbing the mountains of accomplishment. We learn to play ball, decide whether we're cut out for president or dog catcher, and get the best mate we can. Typically we push our boundaries past the edges of our limits. We can know we've gone too far only by going too far! Thus we calibrate our potentials for success and disaster. But there is danger on the Mountains of Accomplishments. We may develop the Atlas Syndrome, taking on our shoulders too many burdens from our worlds of work and home, carrying the weight of these worlds alone, never speaking with others about our struggles. We simply steel ourselves to the pain and begin to believe that this is how we are supposed to travel through life, moving bravely from one peak to the next until either our spirits or our bodies collapse. In the middle of our lives we find we have burned out. It is at this point of collapse that many men begin to wonder about leaving the mountains to explore the underground caves of feeling, finally coming to terms with the fact that inner fulfillment is as vital to wholeness as accomplishments are.

Most men discover the emotional world of the caves in the second half of life. Sheer exhaustion or the reality of addiction begins the humbling process of groping in the dark, traveling inward, going lower and slower, trying to recover our hearts. And at first, we feel awkward and unsure.

We men are not well equipped to explore the inner caves of our emotional worlds. Our skills for identifying, expressing, and listening to feelings are poorly developed. Yet you may find that your environment is demanding that you explore the subterranean world of your soul. For instance, your children may have developed behavioral problems to get your attention; your wife could be spending too much money to buy your love; or your friendships have dried up and blown away because real feelings no longer fuel them. And you know that something is deeply out of sync in you: you have vague forebodings, an increasing edginess, a physical illness, or a desire to engage in some kind of addictive behavior. These things alert you to danger.

So it is that one fine day, after a string of poor judgments have caught up with us, we men are ready for the underground caves. Most of us need to get stretched out on life's rack before we'll pick up these tools and wearily begin feeling our way along in the dark. Usually we're ready for the caves only after a few business failures, a divorce or two, or maybe some deaths in the family.

Life has these necessary losses and inevitably they come pounding on our doors. But we can't send the maid to answer for us. Life has to break us before God can make us into something more than we'd settled for—more than we'd expected.

One Christmas Bethyl and I were biking on an Indian reservation in Arizona. During most of the trip I had been groping in the dark caves of my own soul, looking for wholeness, searching for my heart. We rode onto some federal land with a huge sign saying:

U.S. DEPARTMENT OF THE INTERIOR
Bureau of Reclamation

The sign was especially meaningful to me and I felt it was a message from God that my journey inward was the best path to take. To remind myself later of the significance of the message, I had this notice copied on a board that I hung in my counseling office in honor of my own journey to reclaim my masculine soul.

Exercise

Return to the story of Everyman and the Hag of Death. You are Everyman facing a crisis that will shape and strengthen your soul.

Read the following imagination exercise all the way through. Then close your eyes and see the scene unfold in your mind's eye. If possible, have someone read the exercise to you slowly as you imagine the scene with your eyes closed. You may want to practice the Relaxation Exercise in Chapter 1 before you continue this exercise.

Meeting the Hag of Death

You are Everyman. You are climbing a steep mountain trail. As you climb, look around at the countryside. See it clearly. Smell the clean mountain air. . . .

Look up the mountain path before you. You see a wisp of smoke in the distance. Continue to climb the mountain toward the smoke. . . .

You come to a cave. A fire is burning in front of it, and a figure is hunkered down next to the fire. She is wrapped in a black cloak. You know this is the Hag of Death. As she watches you approach the cave, she draws in the dirt with a stick. She does not smile as you approach. . . .

A shiver runs down your spine. You take a deep breath and let all of the tension flow out of your body. . . . You stop and stand before the Hag. She stands and points to her drawing in the dirt. Lying beside the half-finished drawing is the stick she was using. You stoop to examine the drawing carefully. . . . It is blurry and confusing, but as you concentrate the lines slowly become clear. . . . It is a half-finished picture, an abstract design of your soul. Examine this drawing carefully. . . .

Instinctively you know that you must complete the drawing yourself. You have come to the cave on the mountain to take your soul back. If you successfully finish the drawing, you will continue your journey with your soul as your guide and companion. If you don't, the Hag will finish it and then she will own your soul.

You pick up the stick and begin to finish the drawing. . . . Watch very carefully what you draw. . . . Burn the finished drawing in your memory. . . .

Now look at the Hag. She may have something to say to you. Let her speak and listen carefully to whatever she has to say. . . .

Open your eyes and open your journal. Sketch the completed picture, or design, of your soul.

When you have finished your sketch, record your feelings about drawing your soul. How does it feel to have a picture of your soul? What does your picture tell you about your self? What does the picture tell you about what you need to do on your recovery journey?

If the Hag spoke to you, record what she said.

Return to the picture of your soul that you sketched in your journal as often as you like. Pray with it. Ask God to care for your soul, grow your soul, heal your soul, rejoice with your soul. In other words, ask God for whatever you feel your soul needs.

You may also return to this sketch as a visual reminder that your soul journeys with you in recovery, that your conscious, rational mind is not alone. Your soul is both a guide and a companion.

You can return to your sketch and expand, contract, or alter the drawing at different points along your recovery journey. You may eventually want to draw a completely different picture/design that reflects your transformation in recovery.

Living Well in My Spirit

God speaks to us most often in quiet ways. He whispers in a still, small voice that is heard only by those adventurous souls who are exploring their inner caves. He speaks to us through dreams, feelings, and even through the chronic tension in our bodies. But we men are usually too busy climbing mountains rather than in our inner caves quietly listening for God's voice.

One of the more unfamiliar definitions of sin in the Bible comes from a Hebrew word that means "a failure to listen." When we fail to listen, we are cut off from whoever is speaking to us. If we do not learn to listen to our family of self, we isolate our thoughts from our feelings, our addictive impulses from restraint, our feelings from our spirits. We become unconsciously reactive instead of consciously reflective.

The poet Rainer Maria Rilke elegantly describes his struggle to explore his own inner cave:

> When we win it's with small things,
> And the triumph itself makes us small.
> What is extraordinary and eternal
> Does not want to be bent by us.
> I mean the Angel who appeared
> To the wrestler of the Old Testament:
> When the wrestler's sinews
> Grew long like metal strings,
> He felt them under his fingers
> Like chords of deep music.
>
> Whoever was beaten by this Angel
> (Who often simply declined the fight)
> Went away proud and strengthened
> And great from that harsh hand,
> That kneaded him as if to change his shape.
> Winning does not tempt that man.
> This is how he grows: by being defeated,
> Decisively, by constantly greater beings.[1]

Exercise

You might find it helpful to complete the Relaxation Exercise in Chapter 1 before you begin this exercise. Then close your eyes and imagine God standing next to you. Spend as much time as you like imagining God next to you. Feel his presence. . . .

Ask God for his companionship with your spirit on your recovery journey. Listen carefully to whatever God may wish to say to you in response. . . .

Now tell God how hard it is to be a man in recovery. You may want to tell him about an area of your life that is particularly painful right now. You may want to tell him any doubts you have about healing or recovery. Be as honest as you can. God respects and loves honest men. Listen very carefully for any response God makes, and without interrupting the sensation of God's presence, quietly record his response in your journal.

Next, tell God what is most precious to you on your recovery journey. This may be your family, your work, your own inner child, or living each day clean and sober. Tell God about whatever or whoever it is that brings you deep, lasting joy. . . . Thank God for this precious blessing. . . . Listen carefully, quietly for God's response, and then record it in your journal.

Finally, thank God for this time of honest talk. Ask him to bless your journal and your recovery. Open your eyes and close your journal.

Return frequently to this exercise. Honest, thankful conversations with God about being a man in recovery are crucial to your healing. God is waiting and wanting to help you in your masculine journey of recovering your body, soul, and spirit.

Tactics for Journaling

Take Your Pain Seriously

Usually it is some kind of physical or emotional pain, the kind that addiction can no longer anesthetize, that pushes us to begin recovering our bodies, souls, and spirits. When you are in pain, take it seriously. Under no circumstances should you dismiss or trivialize it. Your pain will lead you to recovery and healing. Marcel Proust wrote that "pain is the most heeded of doctors: To goodness and wisdom we only make promises; *we obey pain.*"[2] Such pain is often a signal that you need to write in your journal in search of healing.

Take Yourself Seriously

Once you take your pain seriously, you will be able to take yourself seriously. That means you must constantly engage in activities that nourish your soul, spirit, and body. Since we men usually operate off the principle of "women and children first" and we haven't been encouraged to develop self-nourishing skills, we often get left behind with no knowledge of how to take care of ourselves.

Writing in your journal on a regular basis is a self-nourishing activity. Even if you are able to nourish yourself in other ways, journaling is one of the most nourishing activities you can undertake. And if it is all you can manage, it will make an important difference in your recovery journey.

Make a regular appointment on your calendar to write in your journal. Once you have a regularly scheduled time, reserve a private place where you'll be undisturbed. Hopefully, such a place or room will reflect your personality and be a place of comfort.

One man I know gets up in the mornings before the rest of the family to be alone and nourish himself with his journal. Another friend finds that his lunch hour at his workplace is the best time and place to lock out the rest of the world and have some time for quiet reflection. Another man goes home from work and, after greeting everyone, disappears into his bedroom for half an hour to spend some time with himself and his journal. As we discussed in Chapter 1, you'll want to think carefully about the place and time, and if you need to, you can change your appointment with your self until you've found the right time and place. But always keep your appointment. Just as your body needs regular nourishment, your soul and spirit need your serious attention to their nourishment. Journaling may be your first step toward taking your self seriously.

Take Your Sacrifices Seriously

Journaling requires a sacrifice of your time and a willingness to struggle and explore the caves of your heart. Remember that sacrifice has redemptive value—you will know the joy in transformation, the pleasure of healing, and the excitement that comes from deep exploration.

A museum in Florence, Italy, has a long hallway leading to a domed area at the end. Pairs of marble chunks are on the left and right. At first the marble looks like unshaped chunks of rock, but when you look closer, you see the crude form of a man, anguished and astonished, struggling to be free of the marble. Each subsequent chunk reveals a little more of the man, and a little less rock. A man is being agonizingly chiseled from the marble. At the end of the hall, centered in the brilliantly lit dome, is the final product of that struggle. Michelangelo's *David* stands there in magnificent perfection.

All of us have the experience depicted by the marble sculptures. We get chiseled, sandpapered, and sculpted, but we are not inert pieces of marble shaped only by outside forces. King David in his life and statue was the product of submission to life's chiseling, sandpapering, and reductions. This long journey from unformed chunk to sculpted man frees each of us, as it did David, from unnecessary trappings. A man's journal is both fire and chisel, a tool in the service of lightening the load. The more time you give the honest chisel to work, the less illusion remains. Journaling sandpapers the veneer and delaminates the high gloss of appearances until you get to the quick of the matter. You begin to see your self as others see you—as God sees you. Indeed "you will know the truth, and the truth will set you free" (but first it will make you miserable!).[3]

Take Your Failures Seriously

You know now that the recovery journey has its ups and downs. Recovery brings healing, but there are also set-backs along the way. The same is true for journaling. Sometimes there are days and weeks when I am crushed by the tyranny of the urgent and I fail to write in my journal at all. Eventually, though, I do return to my journal and begin again. You will also find times when you fail to use your journal as a tool for healing in your recovery. But after a few weeks have elapsed, and you haven't even opened your journal, don't give up. Take your failure seriously. Learn from it, and begin again.

What motivates me to begin writing in my journal after a long absence from it is usually an experience of failure in another part of my life. C. S. Lewis said, "God whispers to us in our pleasure and shouts in our pain."[4] Often the pain of failure in my recovery, a significant relationship, or in my work is what makes me open my journal to search again for healing.

I find that taking my failures seriously and learning from them is a three step process. First, I must forgive myself, for without forgiving myself, it is impossible to begin again. Next, I try to figure out what happened—how I failed in a particular area of my life. I look at the situation or relationship from as many different angles as I can to see what I can learn from my failure. Finally, I simply forge ahead again. There is no need to dwell endlessly on what went wrong. Forging ahead means continuing the journey toward the possibilities of growth and recovery. Forgive, figure, and forge ahead. Following these three steps will help you learn from and grow in failure. And what better place to work through these three steps than in your journal? Your journal is the best tool you have to help you pick your self up, dust your self off, and continue on your journey.

Take a Friend Seriously

It's a good idea to have a trusted friend with whom you can share your journal. This is especially important for men. Sharing your journal with a friend will provide you with encouragement and accountability. Both are critical ingredients in the recovery process. Most men don't court friendships with other men in the same way women make friends with women. We men usually have male friends with whom we share "shop and jock" talk. But in these friendships the activities we talk about and share are more important than the relationship itself. For example, I'm an L. A. Lakers fan. If one friend cancels on going to a game with me, I'll just call another guy and another until I find someone who can go. The game is bigger than the guy. However, other men are more than acquaintances. They are genuine friends. If one of them is not able to go to the game, but wants to spend time being with me anyway, I'll cancel my plans to go to the game. In this case, the guy is bigger than the game.

I have five levels of conversation and interaction with different male friends, each level indicating a deeper level of friendship. The first level indicates typical communication between superficial acquaintances;

the fifth level indicates communication between best friends. These five communication levels are clues to the significance of various male relationships in my life:

Level 1.   Exchange of cliches: "How 'bout them Lakers!"

Level 2.   Exchange of facts: "I've never journaled before."

Level 3.   Exchange of opinions: "I think politics is interesting."

Level 4.   Exchange of feelings: "I hate it when my wife clams up on me."

Level 5.   Exchange of relationship statements: "Here's how I see you and me; how do you feel about our friendship?"

If you have a Level 5 friendship, a best friend, share your journal with him. Knowing that you share your recovery journey with a fellow traveler gives your writing an added dimension of joy and excitement. On a regular basis, either once a week or once a month, make a date to have breakfast with your Level 5 friend. Both of you must agree that it will be a time to talk about the honest feelings you discovered as you were journaling, and that it will be a time for your friend to give you honest feedback. You will give him honest feedback, too, for hopefully he will be keeping a journal also.

When you get together, begin by sharing the more superficial parts of your lives. After a little while, begin to go deeper, but go slowly. Don't share all of your most personal thoughts and dreams first thing. Let that develop gradually. This is not a contest! Trusting each other with your important parts takes time and courage. Meeting regularly over time with such a friend will give you both the courage you need to continue your journeys of self-exploration and recovery.

Exercise

Open your journal. Before writing, think a moment about your present male relationships. Ask yourself, do I have a male friend—someone who is more than an acquaintance, someone with whom I can talk seriously about life and faith? Even if you've never had a serious conversation with one of your friends, pick the one you think would most likely respond to you and begin writing in your journal about this friendship. Review your relationship with him, and answer these questions in your journal:

- How did you first meet each other?

- How did the relationship develop?

- Describe how this friendship feels to you. How much do you value it and why? What would your life be like if this man were not a part of it?

- Does one of you put more work into the relationship than the other? If so, how?

- What has sustained and deepened your commitment to each other?

- How often do you get together? When you get together, what activities do you share?

- What have been the most enjoyable/difficult times you've gone through together?

- Do you feel this friendship is the kind that would allow you to occasionally share excerpts from your journal with your friend?

Perhaps you have many male acquaintances, but no real friend. Many men today don't have real friendships. Think for a moment about a relationship with another man that almost developed into a friendship. Write a letter in your journal to this almost friend. Explain to him why your acquaintance didn't develop into a friendship. Some of your reasons might be that you were too busy; you felt awkward; you enjoyed being with women more than men; you always felt that you have to compete with other men; you didn't seem to have the words or skills you need to transform an acquaintance into a friend;

you sensed he was unwilling to make a friendship. Once you finish your letter, date and sign it.

Re-read your letter. Ask yourself if there is someone among your male acquaintances with whom you might develop a friendship. If there is, write the person's name in your journal. Underneath his name, write two things you can do over the next two weeks to begin a real friendship. You could invite him to have breakfast or to go jogging or you could call him on the phone to catch up on what he is doing, and so on.

It may be that you are not ready to work on developing a male friendship. Return to this exercise and do it again.

Remember, boys are born from women, but men are born from men. If you have the opportunity to join a men's support group, do it. I've been leading a men's group since 1985, and during this time we have regularly shared our journals with the group. We call ourselves "the Paternity Ward," because we help give birth to the man in one another.

Whether you share your journal with just one good friend or with a men's support group, you will find that sharing your inner journey with other men will be a most rewarding part of your recovery.

Summary

In this chapter you have explored some of the differences between men and women in recovery. You have learned how to use your journal in the masculine journey of recovering your body, soul, and spirit. You have also examined the importance of male friendship to your recovery. And you have learned that your journal is the best tool you have in taking yourself seriously as a recovering man.

You may find your self returning to this chapter again and again. That's great! The excitement of our journeys comes from the knowledge that we never stop growing or healing or recovering.

6

Journaling

for

Women

Recovery as Women's Work

Recovery for women is like weaving tapestries of our lives. Healing weaves a pattern in our innermost beings, the inner core, then continues to weave its way into our outer lives. The inner core is where the deep healing of recovery begins. Such healing gradually transforms our inner selves, our relationships with loved ones, and the world in general. As a woman in recovery, you must learn to know your heart and trust it and have confidence to champion your healing.

If the recovery process can be likened to a tapestry, the strength for weaving the tapestry comes from drinking healing waters. Jeremiah describes a tree "planted by the waters,/Which spreads out its roots by the river,/And will not fear when heat comes;/But its leaf will be green,/And will not be anxious in the year of drought,/Nor will cease from yielding fruit" (Jer. 17:8). When you are connected to the healing in your heart and to God who heals your heart, you are able to run your life and shape your relationships from the inside out—not the outside in. God offers a healing stream to feed your heart and make you confident, even while the outside world tries to thwart your recovery. Too often we women are challenged to set aside our own healing to fulfill the demands or obligations of others—and we find ourselves in places of drought, cut off from what we need to renew and strengthen ourselves. Recovery for women is healing that comes from the inside out. We sink our roots deep into the healing stream God gives to us so we can survive and thrive even in a land of drought.

The recovery journey for women means returning again and again to the waters that nourish us. In this chapter you will learn to use your journal as a portable well, a place where God offers you healing waters to nourish and strengthen you for the journey.

Your journal is a place where you can learn to see your self, God, and others clearly. When your life is filled with well-meaning busyness, it is difficult to read the signs of your recovery. But spending regular time with your journal slows you down so you can read those signs. Journaling helps you stop, look, and listen for the signs God gives you on your recovery journey. In *The Narnia Chronicles*, C. S. Lewis writes: "First, remember, remember, remember the signs. Say them to yourself when you awake in the morning and when you lie down at night, and when you wake in the middle of the night. And whatever strange things may happen to you, let nothing turn your mind from following the signs. . . . Remember the signs and believe in the signs. Nothing else matters."[1]

Your journal is a place to record the signs God gives you in your family of self and your dreams, relationships, struggles, and joys. Such signs point the way toward healing.

When you journal regularly, you will be nourished and strengthened. You learn to follow the signs of your recovery. And you discover you have choices about which direction to take on your journey. Your journal helps you explore the choices life offers so you can make decisions confidently. In your journal, you recover the joy of making choices for your life.

Feeling nourished, reading signs, and making healthy choices are parts of living wisely. Your journal is a tool to help you become a wise woman.

The Search for Wisdom

In the Bible, wisdom is represented as a woman. In Proverbs and Psalms wisdom is an elusive woman, more precious than jewels, stronger than physical or military strength, hidden in dark, mysterious places, but always available to those with the courage to search for her.

The Old Testament name for wisdom is Sophia. She is a practical guide to life and to God. Sophia usually lives in the dark places of our hearts. Often during times of suffering and darkness she travels to our conscious minds to guide and strengthen us.

The following story illustrates how wisdom is born in our lives. Read the story carefully and then complete the exercise that follows it.

The Wise Moon Mother

Once upon a time wisdom was believed to be a kindly Moon Mother who cared very much for people on earth. When the Moon Mother was in her fullest phase in the sky, the villagers, who lived on the edge of a great forest, could walk safely at night without falling into dangerous bogs. But when the Moon Mother was empty, hidden in darkness each month, the villagers knew it was not safe to leave their homes at night. They knew the forest would be too dark, and dangerous forest creatures would be on the prowl.

One night, when the Moon Mother was in her phase of darkness, an old, silver-haired woman began a journey into the forest. The Moon Mother continued to hide behind her cloak of darkness and it was very dark indeed. The woman was very old, but she was very brave. She entered the dark forest with a lamp held high in her right hand. As the night wore on, and as she journeyed deeper into the forest, her lamp began to dim. The woman realized her lamplight would soon be gone and that she was quite lost.

Vines began twining themselves around the old woman's ankles. Little nasty forest creatures bit her legs. At last the lamp went dark and she stepped into a bog. Quicksand began to slowly pull her down.

The old woman was about to give up hope when she raised her eyes and saw a sliver of light. The Moon Mother had come to earth. Though she walked with her dark cloak wrapped tightly about her, occasionally the light would escape. The Moon Mother walked to the bog where the old woman was struggling. She grasped the woman by the hand and lifted her to safety.

The Moon Mother carried the old woman to the top of a little hill. There she sat down, holding the old woman in her arms, rocking slowly and gently, and murmuring soothing sounds to quiet the old woman's fear. The old woman fell asleep. As the night deepened and Moon Mother continued to rock her, the old woman began to change. Soon she had become middle aged, the lines of care barely etched in her face. A little later, the woman was young with strong, supple limbs. Just before dawn, as the Moon Mother began to disappear in a vaporous cloud, the old woman had become a beautiful girl toddler.

The sun was just beginning to rise when the Moon Mother plucked three hairs from the toddler's head and threw them against the roots of an old oak tree. As each hair hit the tree, it made a little sound: Ping! Ping! Ping! At that moment the Moon Mother disappeared. Awakened by the sound, the toddler jumped to her feet and, laughing in the sunshine, ran home.

Wisdom is God's gift to us. Wisdom lives somewhere inside each of us. Journaling is a wonderful way to search and embrace the wisdom hidden in your soul. In the exercise that follows, make the story of the Moon Mother your own story of your search for wisdom.

Exercise

Open your journal to a fresh page. Label the top of the page "The Wise Moon Mother." Choose a particular detail from the story that grabbed your attention. You may choose to be a person, the forest, a nasty forest creature, the lamp—anything you wish. Pretend you are the person or thing you have selected from the story.

Begin writing in your journal as the person or thing from the story. Remember to use first person, present tense. Record any thoughts or feelings you have as you write. For example:

I am the lamp the old woman holds in the dark forest. It is hard work to make my light shine in so much darkness. But it is a joy to help this old woman, who is my friend.

After you have written as much as you can about being a person or thing from the story, write another paragraph or two about what you learned from being that person or thing. Write about how you will apply what you learned to your recovery. For example:

I learned from the lamp that my recovery illuminates the darkness. Sometimes recovery is hard work for me. But when I am good to myself, and shed as much light on my journey as I can, I help illuminate the way for my friends and loved ones.

Applying the lessons you learn in your recovery is practicing wisdom. Return to this exercise as often as you like, becoming a different part of the Wise Moon Mother story each time. You will identify a different wise part of yourself to help you in recovery.

Wisdom is not new to you. You have been growing in wisdom and experience for years. The following exercise helps you search for glimpses of wisdom in your past to help you in the present.

In preparation for writing this chapter, I gathered around me several journals I have completed over the years. As I reviewed what I had written, I was comforted to see Jesus' words in my journals and to notice how he has woven his presence into my journey.

I read a few paragraphs from an old journal to Vance. They recorded my thoughts about him as our relationship grew and deepened. Both our spirits were touched as I shared my old writings in these new times. I gleaned new, wise insights into my present journey with Vance from experiences and lessons learned long ago.

You have a history of wisdom, too.

Exercise

Search your house and assemble old journals, diaries, letters, books with notes in the margins or underlined sentences, or scrapbooks.

Schedule an appointment with your self to review these records of your past. You don't have to read every word or sentence you've written or collected, but you need to give your self plenty of time to skim the material, stopping to read only what attracts your attention. Keep your present journal next to you. As you come across material that grabs you, jot in your present journal the event, thought, feeling, relationship, or memory it brings to your mind.

When you are finished reviewing your old journals or other past material, go back to the notations you made in your present journal. Are there any pearls of wisdom you discovered in your past journals? If so, write about them, especially how you will apply these pearls of wisdom to your recovery.

Sorting Out Your Feelings

Maturity for women in the recovery process is marked by clarity. We need to see ourselves and others in our world clearly. That means we regularly sort out the feelings that lie underneath our thoughts, perceptions, and values. Using your journal regularly to sort out your feelings will enable you to gain confidence in your identity as a woman; establish healthy boundaries in important relationships; discover new talents, skills, and capabilities; and help you make wise, positive choices.

The following exercise is designed to help you sort out your feelings and get a clearer picture of your self and your life.

Exercise

Open your journal to a fresh page and label the top "Sorting Out." If you are writing in your journal in the morning, think about your schedule, the people, and the activities for the day to come. If it is evening, review the people and activities of the day just past.

Select an activity, event, or person from your day and write it near the top of the page. Then write a couple of paragraphs describing how you really feel about that person, event, or activity.

Next write another couple of paragraphs that explain how your feelings shape that particular relationship, event, or activity. Ask your self what impact your feelings have on this particular part of your world.

Finally, ask your self what these feelings tell you about your self and your recovery. Ask your self: Do these feelings tell me I like my self? How do I express these feelings in a healthy, appropriate way? What are these feelings telling me to do about which direction in life to take?

Return to this exercise whenever your life feels cluttered and you want to see clearly again.

Experiencing Power in Recovery

Women in recovery must always struggle with power issues. Our dysfunctional family lives have taught us that we are powerless, helpless victims. But God does not call us to remain victims. We women on healing journeys must recover power in our lives—not the kind of power that manipulates or abuses others, but the kind of power that gives us the nourishment and energy to live as the healthy persons God intends us to be. The Bible offers several examples of powerful women who used their power to live healthy lives that glorified God. We can learn a great deal from their stories that we can use in our own lives.

Deborah was a prophetess and ruler in Israel. She was a clear, logical planner, who used her political and military power wisely. And she was an honest, straight-talker, who wasn't afraid to be direct in dealing with others. She knew what she wanted for herself and her people, and she achieved her goals. (See Judges 4.)

Abigail was also a strong woman. She was a housewife who was married for years to an alcoholic. He was no good at sniffing out danger or identifying problems, so, like a good co-dependent, Abigail would perpetually bail her husband out of trouble. Finally, Abigail's alcoholic husband drank himself to death. Abigail wanted a better life for herself in her next marriage and used her feminine powers to attract and marry King David. (See 1 Samuel 25–30.)

Jocabed, like the rest of her family, was a Hebrew enslaved to the ruling Egyptians. When she learned that all male Hebrew babies were to be killed, Jocabed did a brave and powerful thing. She covered her infant son with prayers and left him in a basket on a river. Eventually, the baby boy was found by an Egyptian princess, and Jocabed offered to be the baby's wet-nurse. Jocabed's son, Moses, grew up to be the greatest leader the Hebrew people had ever known. More importantly, Moses became the friend of God—all because his mother used her love and power to risk everything to save him. (See Exodus.)

Mary was a young teenager engaged to be married to a much older man. During her engagement, Mary became pregnant, and her fiancé's family wanted to put her away. But Mary's power was expressed in her quiet acceptance of God's promise to her about the baby she carried. Later, as Jesus grew up, her faith was powerful enough to let him go his own way and pursue the mission God had given him. Mary's power was such that she did not interfere even when Jesus went to his own death.

These biblical women are role models for women in recovery. Each chose to use her personal power in a different way: Deborah used her natural power as a leader. Abigail used her feminine power to make a better, healthier life for herself. Jocabed used the power of motherly love to risk everything for her child. Mary's power was that of quiet faith and acceptance. God wants us to use the power he has placed inside us to bring healing to our lives and relationships.

During our recovery, we may need to call on different kinds of power at different times in our lives. For example, working our recovery in the workplace may mean we need to draw on the kind of power demonstrated by Deborah, but continuing our recovery journey during times of hardship and adversity may mean we need to call upon the power of faith that Mary had.

The following exercise will help you identify your own power. It will show you where in your life you feel strongest and where you feel weakest.

Exercise

Read through this entire exercise before beginning.

Title a new page in your journal "Personal Power," and draw five horizontal lines. Label each line the following way:

Helpless	*My Inner Power Level*	Powerful

Helpless	*My Present Family*	Powerful

Helpless	*My Family of Origin*	Powerful

Helpless	*My Friendships*	Powerful

Helpless	*My Workplace*	Powerful

Use each line as a continuum of how powerful you feel. Place a dot on each line that shows how powerful you feel yourself to be in that situation.

For example, you may feel very powerful personally; therefore, your inner power level line might look like this:

Helpless   *My Inner Power Level*   *Powerful*

But you may feel relatively powerless at work; therefore, your workplace line might look like this:

Helpless   *My Workplace*   *Powerful*

Each one of these lines represents a set of relationships where you use your personal power. The first line is the most important. It indicates how much you feel the good power God has given you. That power can then be expressed in these other areas of your life.

Remember that personal power is a good kind of power. When it is positive it is not manipulative or abusive, but is a source of nourishment and healing in your life. It gives you energy to continue your recovery and build healthy relationships with those you love and the world around you.

After you have finished marking each line, write a paragraph about each one, asking yourself why you feel helpless/powerful in this area. When you are examining a line that indicates feelings of helplessness, ask yourself: What do I need to do in this area to help me feel more powerful? When you are examining a line that indicates feelings of personal power, ask yourself: How does feeling powerful in this area make me feel about myself and my relationships?

Then briefly note the differences you've indicated in personal power levels. For example, you might notice you feel you have a lot of personal power, but your present family line indicates you feel relatively helpless. Ask yourself why there is such discrepancy between these lines. How can you begin to use your personal power in such a way that you can feel more powerful at home?

Return to this exercise periodically to take an inventory of your power levels in various areas in your life. Remember, recovering your personal power fuels your recovery in general.

I most often experience personal strength and power when I have intense feelings and my journal reflects this. When I have intense feelings, my pen moves boldly, often rapidly across the page. Sometimes I get so carried away, writing so furiously, that my pen tears the paper.

At other times, when my personal power is at an ebb, I feel sick, hurt, or fragile in some way and writing in my journal at all is difficult. But when I do, the pen moves slowly; the writing is much more subdued.

It is a good thing to experience the strength of our power because it often fuels our recovery. Complete the following exercise whenever you want to feel how strong you really are.

Exercise

Spend a few moments identifying a person, place, activity, object, idea, or event that you feel passionately about. Passionate feelings are very strong emotions of joy, grief, pleasure, rage, intense curiosity, and so forth.

Once you've identified someone or something you feel passionate about, write a letter in your journal to that person, object, or activity. This letter is not to be mailed. Write your strongest feelings in the letter. As you write, pay attention to how you are experiencing feelings of personal power.

After you sign and date your letter, write a brief paragraph describing how you experienced your power in this letter.

Experiencing our personal power gives us the energy we need to continue on our recovery journeys. But that power must be channeled into completing constructive tasks that bring healing to our inner selves and our outer relationships. Power is channeled through resolve.

Experiencing Resolve in Your Journal

You know that recovery is not temporary. It requires a life-long commitment to health and wholeness for ourselves and our relationships. Recovery may be understood as a series of tasks, goals, and challenges that life sets before us which we must handle in healthy, responsible, appropriate ways. Recovery demands resolve. Resolve marries our personal power with our will or drive. Marrying power with will gives us the ability to complete any task set before us, to take on any challenge. Resolve channels our personal power to "keep on keeping on." Having firm resolve means we take initiative and action in our recovery.

The ancient Greeks told a story that illustrates what it means to have resolve on a journey of recovery:

Psyche's Recovery Journey

There once was a beautiful young woman named Psyche. Her soul had been stolen from her and was locked away in the underworld. To recover her soul, Psyche would have to complete four seemingly impossible tasks.

She was told that when she crossed the River Styx into the underworld, she would meet several persons. All of these people would attempt to distract Psyche from her recovery task. She was warned that the people she met would be surprising. One might appear as a wounded child, pleading for help. Another might be an attractive, seductive man. Yet another might be a terrifying woman.

Psyche was instructed not to listen to any of them. She was to harden her heart to any person who would distract her. If Pysche listened to any one of the tempting people she would meet, and her resolve to complete her recovery journey failed her, she would remain forever in the underworld.

As a woman, developing and experiencing your resolve means disciplining your emotional world, your power, and your will to focus on the various challenges and goals of recovery. Many people, things, or activities would interrupt your recovery. Even your own emotional life attempts to sabotage your journey (for example, feelings of hopelessness or acute depression sometimes tempt you to abandon recovery). The following exercise will help you identify that which would tempt you from completing your recovery journey.

Exercise

Open your journal and label a fresh page "Keeping My Resolve," and then write the answers to these questions.

1. Do you sometimes daydream? What does it feel like to drift into daydreams? Write about the times when you most enjoy daydreaming. Then write about how this may sometimes distract you in your recovery.

2. Do you have many good ideas or plans? Do you often put your ideas or plans into action? If so, write about how an idea put into action furthered your recovery. If you have difficulty putting ideas into action, describe why that may be hard for you to do.

3. What kinds of tasks do you finish easily? Do these tasks help you along in your recovery journey? What kinds of tasks are difficult to finish, but easy to abandon? (A telling response to this set of questions may be: "I finish doing stuff for my kids, but the things I want to do for myself never get done.")

4. How strong is your resolve when you have set a goal for yourself to complete in recovery? Does your resolve last or does it disappear over time? Do you have anyone, like a sponsor, to encourage your resolve?

5. How much of a risk-taker are you? Do you like risk or do you prefer caution when setting goals and approaching tasks? Write a couple of paragraphs describing your feelings about risk and how those feelings impact your recovery.

After answering these questions, choose one goal you want to achieve that will have an impact on your recovery. Write that goal in your journal. Then think about when you want to achieve this goal. Choose the date and write it next to your goal. Beneath the goal, write three tasks you will need to complete to achieve it and give each task a target completion date. When you begin to work on these tasks to achieve your goal, keep a record of your progress in your journal, writing about your experiences and feelings as you work toward completing your goal.

Return to this exercise anytime you feel the need to strengthen your resolve in recovery. It is a very good idea to periodically write goals and tasks for recovery in your journal. Your journal holds you accountable for finishing what you start.

Summary

In this chapter you have learned why journaling is important for women in recovery. Journaling helps you in your search for wisdom, healing, and nourishment. Your journal is also useful to you in sorting out your feelings, experiencing your power, and practicing your resolve.

Let your journal be a place where, like Psyche, you journey to recover your soul.

The
Couple's
Journal

Couples and Healthy Families

It is almost impossible to recover from any kind of substance abuse or dysfunction alone. We must have a set of supportive relationships to work a recovery program successfully. Family relationships have the power to help or hurt our recovery. People who are isolated from healthy family relationships run the greatest risk of abandoning their recovery programs. Being a part of a healthy family gives us support and care to continue recovery.

The building block of a healthy family is the couple around whom that family is created and formed. If you care about the health and well-being of your family, explore your life as a couple. Your relationship as a couple guides and sustains other family relationships.

It may be that you are not married, but still are part of a couple. You may be thinking about marriage or are very involved in a relationship. Whether you are a married couple, with or without children, or partici-pate in a significant relationship with another person, this chapter is for you. Either one or both of you may be recovering from an addiction or dysfunction.

You will explore writing in your journal as an individual and as a couple. This chapter will help you understand your life as a couple, help you build intimacy in your relationship, and help repair damage that happens to the relationship. Journaling for couples helps you shape a sturdy *we* on your recovery journey together, rather than each traveling alone as a fragile, isolated *me*.

A Story from Our Marriage

There were several reasons I wanted to marry Vance. One was I felt I could be totally honest in expressing my thoughts and feelings to him. He was rarely threatened by anything I had to say. Through the years I have appreciated his ability to hear me, respect me, and love me, especially during those times when we disagreed.

There have been times, though, when our ability to communicate lovingly and honestly has broken down. During one such period of time, our exasperation with each other reached a peak. Our ability to listen to each other was completely blocked. It felt like all the powers of evil in the world were trying to separate us. As a wife, I felt pressed to my absolute limits.

I poured out my pain and frustration in my journal. Then I did something I had never done before. I handed my journal to Vance and asked him to read what I had written. Vance read *me*, and my body experienced a great sense of relief. Then he picked up his pen and wrote in my journal, telling me how he felt about what he had read there. That started us on a process of writing in each other's journals, emptying our hearts in an attempt to establish communication once again. When I read Vance's journal, I often cried. But my tears were for the pain he was experiencing.

I heard what I hadn't been able to hear from Vance with my ears through our writing in and exchanging journals. Our journals became our ears. Writing in each other's journals worked for us when all our other skills in living together as a couple failed. Eventually, our hearts began to knit themselves together once again.

Different Kinds of Couple's Journals

There are several kinds of couple's journals. Experiment with some of the following suggestions to discover the kind of journal you both will enjoy working with.

You can share with your partner selections from your private journal. You maintain your privacy as individuals by choosing to read aloud, or copy on another piece of paper, those journal entries you want to share with your partner.

A less conventional journal involves letters and notes. Write letters and mail them to each other. Put Post-it notes for each other on the refrigerator door. Write notes, and then crumple them and put them in each other's socks. Eventually all these notes and letters are collected by each partner and put in a scrapbook. The scrapbook is your couple's journal and becomes a record of your life together.

You may want to create a special journal to use as a couple. It could be a loose-leaf binder to which the two of you add and subtract pages of writings, drawings, photos, or collages. Or you may want to use a bound blank book in which you take turns reading and writing. Whenever an entry is made by one of you in this journal, you will need to signal your partner that there is something new to see. Of course, you may simply tell each other to go have a look, but experiment with being creative! Put your couple's journal under your spouse's pillow. Put a fanciful note on the bathroom mirror. Hang a red cap on the front door knob. Leave a clever message on the answering machine. Remember that keeping a couple's journal should be fun as well as work.

Whatever form of couple's journal you choose, be sure to keep it in a safe place away from the curious eyes of children or guests. I know a couple who put a lock on their journal. Each partner has a key.

Intimacy and Your Journal

Have you ever awakened in the morning, looked over at your sleeping spouse, and wondered: Who is this person? You may have spent years together, but he or she seems more of a mystery now than ever before. In fact, your spouse may be more of a stranger than you care to admit.

Developing intimacy is a process of exploring the mystery in each other. The following exercises are designed to help you develop intimacy by exploring the mysteries in each other. During these exercises you will learn to slow down and savor each other like a fine, foreign meal. I find that I appreciate and love Bethyl even more when I slow down to question, understand, and enjoy her. If I am to develop intimacy with her, I must learn about the people, places, and situations that have shaped this woman that I love.

Before beginning any of the exercises, first read all of them. Then decide which one you both want to work on. Not all exercises will be appropriate for the relationship you have just now. Choose to work with the one that fits best for both of you.

A Couple's Dance

Partners in a couple conduct their relationship like a dance. There are three basic dance steps they use when relating with each other:

1. Each moves *toward* the other seeking intimacy and union.
2. Each moves *against* the other when there is conflict.
3. Each moves *away* from the other as individuals leading their own lives.

Healthy couples have all three dance steps in their relationship. Such healthy couples are able to communicate which step they are using in their relationship at any given time. The following exercise is designed to help you identify these steps and talk about them with your partner.

Exercise

Each of you write an ending for the following sentences:

- I move toward you when . . .
- I move against you when . . .
- I move away from you when . . .

After completing each sentence, jot down a couple of examples from your relationship that explains it.

When you are both finished writing, take turns reading aloud your sentences and examples.

Discuss the following questions:

- Which step are both of you best at as a couple? Why? Which step are you best at as individuals? Why?

- Which step gives you the most difficulty in your relationship as a couple? Why? Which step gives you the most difficulty as an individual? Why?

To complete this exercise, each of you write in your couple's journal an ending for the following sentence:

- What I love most about you is . . .

Then each read aloud what the other has written.

Parents and Couples

A couple's relationship often includes a variety of relational styles they each learned from their parents. Healthy couples are aware that their relationship may contain six people—you and me and two sets of parents. We learned how to relate to other people when we were children as we watched and imitated how our parents related to each other and the world around them. As we grew up, we learned what a marriage should look like largely based on what we saw in our parents' relationship. If our family of origin was dysfunctional, we learned from our parents what we did *not* want in a significant relationship.

Whether we liked what we saw in our parents' relationship or whether we never wanted to imitate their relationship, the ways our parents conducted their relationship unconsciously continue to creep into our own lives. The following exercise is designed to help you identify your parents' ways of conducting their relationship as a couple. Once you get a clear picture of your parents' relational style, you and your partner may want to discuss how parental styles are active in your life together as a couple.

Exercise

Either take turns writing in your couple's journal, or write on separate pieces of paper or in your personal journals. Answer the following questions, but don't read each other's responses. You will share your answers verbally toward the end of the exercise.

1. In general, which one of your parents "wore the pants" in the family? In other words, who was in charge of your parents'

marriage? How did the less dominant parent respond to the one in control?

2. How did your parents say no to each other? Did they say no directly or indirectly? Was one more direct than the other? If so, how?

3. Did either of your parents consistently avoid accepting responsibility by blaming the other? If so, which one? Give an example.

4. In general, how did your parents handle conflict between them? Did they express conflict through loud arguments or by not speaking to each other? Did they hide conflict from the children? Did one or both of them abuse alcohol or another substance? Did they have other ways of expressing or dealing with conflict? If so what were they?

5. How did your parents let each other know they were valued and loved? How did they express affectionate feelings?

6. Describe your mother's style of relating to your father. How is her style at work in the way you relate to your partner?

7. Describe your father's style of relating to your mother. How is his style at work in the way you relate to your partner?

8. What did you admire about your parents' relationship?

9. What did you dislike about your parents' relationship?

10. How do you see your parents' relationship styles active in your own couple's relationship?

11. What did you learn from your parents that is helpful in your life as part of a couple? What did you learn from your parents that is harmful to your life as a couple?

After you have written your answers individually, exchange them and each read aloud the other's answers.

Close this exercise by having a general discussion about what you learned from it. Focus especially on aspects of your parents' relationship, and what you have learned from your parents you would like to erase from your life together.

This exercise may trigger an on-going discussion. Feel free to return to any portion of it to discuss your answers more completely.

We also learned at our parents' knees what it means to be a man or a woman. Our parents taught us what they felt was appropriate feminine or masculine behavior as part of a couple. The following exercise will help both of you identify what you learned about being a man or woman from your same sex parent. Again, whatever you learned from your parents is often imported into your life together as a couple.

Exercise

You will complete this exercise individually and then share your writing with each other.

In your couple's journal, private journals, or on separate sheets of paper, write a letter to your same sex parent. If you are a man, write to your father; if you are a woman, write to your mother. It does not matter whether your parent is living or dead—you will not mail this letter.

Imagine the face of your same sex parent. Hear him or her calling your name. If you have difficulty clearly imagining your parent, find a picture of him or her and put it in front of you as you write.

After you have a clear picture of your parent in your mind's eye, write a letter to him or her in which you tell what you learned from him or her about being a man or a woman in a couple.

Once you have stated what you learned, tell that parent how you feel about what you learned. Be as honest as possible in expressing your feelings about what you learned from him or her. Begin by telling your parent what you most appreciate about learning to be a man or woman. Use memories of observing your parents' relationship. For example:

Dad, I appreciated you teaching me that a real man doesn't always have to be right in a relationship. You showed me that real, masculine strength lies in being flexible. I remember when you and Mom would argue, you always seemed to know what you could learn from her.

After expressing your appreciation, express any disappointments or hurt about what you learned from your parent. For example:

Mom, I was often a lonely little girl when I saw how lonely you were with Dad. It makes me sad to remember the time you wanted to hold hands with him when you were shopping together, but he put his hands in his pockets. It makes me afraid now to ask for what I want in my marriage.

Finish the letter by telling your parent that you know he or she did his or her best to teach you about being a man or woman. Also tell your parent that you are sorting through what you learned from him or her in your present relationship as a couple. If you feel it is possible to forgive your parent for any shortcomings in this area, do so now. But if forgiveness is not possible just now, come back to it later.

Sign your name and date the letter.

Now exchange letters with your partner and read them silently. If you like, you may discuss the letters together now, or put them away. Should you choose to put them away for a while, pick a time when both of you can look at them again. Then discuss how what you learned from your parents about masculine and feminine behavior impacts your relationship as a couple.

Changing the Rules

Have you ever felt stuck in your life as a couple? Have you ever felt that there was no room to breathe or that your personal lives as individuals were slipping through your fingers? If you answered yes to either question, chances are there are some unwritten or unspoken rules in your relationship that need to be examined, and possibly changed.

In the Bible, the book of Esther gives us an example of a couple whose relationship was threatened by a rule that governed their marriage. Ahasuerus and Esther lived in the town of Susa. They came from very different families: Ahasuerus was from royalty; Esther was from a family of Hebrew slaves. He was powerful financially and politically; she was a powerful beauty with immense spiritual resources.

Their relationship, like yours, had rules that governed their life together. But unlike yours, the rules they lived by were written down as the law of the land. The rule that threatened their relationship as a couple was that Ahasuerus could approach Esther whenever he wanted. But, Esther could not come to Ahasuerus unless first she had his permission. If Esther violated this rule, Ahasuerus had the power to have her killed.

A situation developed that meant Esther had to approach Ahasuerus without his prior permission. At stake were the lives of her Jewish people. Esther risked her life to break a rule that no longer worked for any-one. When she broke that rule, she broke new ground in her marriage as well.

The homes from which you both came may have had unconscious, unwritten rules about behavior. Just the thought of breaking those rules may have made you feel like you were risking your life. Some of those powerful, unwritten rules may have included:

- Always be cheerful, even when you don't feel like it.
- Never confront Dad when he is drinking.
- Always stay with Mom when she is depressed.
- Never talk about what you really feel with anyone else.
- Never talk about what you see at home with anyone else.
- Always be in control, even when you are scared to death.

Such rules have great power. Some of them are so powerful they con-tinue to operate in your adult lives. It is crucial that you both identify the unwritten rules you grew up with, particularly those secret rules that are still operating in your relationship together.

An unwritten, unbreakable rule in my family was: Never discuss how you feel about struggles in the family. It was acceptable to talk about our shared belief in God, but it was unacceptable to discuss our struggles and differences as a family.

This rule applied especially to my brother, Jonathan, who is develop-mentally disabled. We were allowed to thank God for Jon's improve-ments and for the natural health remedies that helped him. But we were not allowed to talk about the painful feelings and suffering that were part of the special burdens involved in having a disabled child in the family.

The impact this unwritten family rule had on my life was powerful. Since I wasn't allowed to discuss how I felt about caring for Jon, I didn't begin dating until I was eighteen years old. I spent my adolescence be-lieving that if I left my brother alone to go on a date, I would be abandon-ing him. So instead of dating, I went places with Jon to keep him from being lonely.

I finally broke this family rule when I married Vance. Since a part of being a healthy married couple required discussing our feelings honestly with each other, I had to learn how to talk openly with Vance about my feelings when we faced struggles in our relationship. It was difficult for me to learn that it was okay to talk about struggles in our family. But I am so glad I did! Honestly discussing my feelings about my relationship with Vance helps me enjoy our life as a couple.

Identifying and changing some of these unwritten, secret family rules may make us feel like we are risking our lives in the same way that Esther risked her life to break an unhealthy rule. But examining the unwritten rules you both live by, and changing the ones that are unhealthy, will bring new life and intimacy into your relationship as a couple.

Exercise

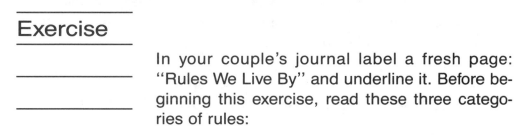

In your couple's journal label a fresh page: "Rules We Live By" and underline it. Before beginning this exercise, read these three categories of rules:

1. There are rules that govern which feelings and expressions of emotion are acceptable/unacceptable.
2. There are rules about how decisions are made in your relationship as a couple. Such as decisions about money, time together and time apart, sexual behavior, children, recreational activities—like TV programs and vacations, and food, such as menus, preparation, how often you eat out, and scheduling meals.
3. There are rules about who sets the emotional mood in the house.

Decide between the two of you who will be the scribe, recording in your couple's journal the rules you are about to identify.

Write the number *one* near the top of the page. Read the first category of rules again, begin identifying and writing rules that determine appropriate feelings and expressions of emotions in your relationship. Do not discuss the rules you write just yet. Merely identify them and record them in your couple's journal. When writing the rules, begin each one with the words *always* or *never*. For example:

Always end the evening with a good night kiss.
Never discuss sad feelings at the dinner table.

Repeat this process for the two remaining rule categories.

When you have completed identifying and recording rules for all three categories, go back and read them aloud one rule at a time. As you read each rule, ask yourselves the following questions:

1. Is this rule healthy for our relationship right now? Why?
2. Is this rule unhealthy for our relationship right now? Why?
3. Does this rule need to be re-written to strengthen our relationship? If you feel it does, re-write it in your couple's journal.
4. Does this rule need to be eliminated to strengthen our relationship? If you feel it does, draw a line through it.

Use these questions to discuss each rule.

Close this exercise by re-reading the rules you have kept or re-written.

Periodically return to this section of your couple's journal to see whether these written rules are working to support and strengthen your relationship. If later you find one or more no longer contribute to your health and happiness as a couple, change or eliminate it.

The Stages of a Couple's Life

Just as individuals move through several stages in life, couples also travel through stages. But couples do not journey through each stage only once. They may re-visit these stages again and again.

This section identifies four stages couples typically travel through in their life together. Following the description of each stage, there is a journal exercise designed for you to use in reflecting on your life as a couple. Remember couples repeat these stages at various times during their life together. Read through this section, then choose the stage you would both like to work on and proceed with completing the exercise.

The Romantic Stage

Each couple goes through an initial romantic stage. In this stage, you can't wait to tell each other all about yourselves. You share with each other your dreams and visions, your past hurts and triumphs, and your feelings for each other. Each of you feels welcomed into the other's presence, and you both feel loved and honored.

It is a good idea for couples to return occasionally to the romantic stage. After you've journeyed through life together, you find you have both changed as individuals. Major changes occur in your life together—children leave home, one of you finishes graduate school, you both change jobs, you move to a new city, a parent dies, a child marries, and so on. After such change, a healthy couple wants to get re-acquainted with each other. An enjoyable way of getting to know each other again is to employ a little romance.

Exercise

Spend a few minutes remembering the time when you first met. Then take turns writing letters to each other in your couple's journal. Write about the memory and about how you felt when you were discovering each other. Your letter might begin like this:

Dear _____,
    I remember when you touched my skin and told me how soft I was. I felt so accepted. You sat next to me for more than an hour and listened to me tell you about my work. I felt very important to you.

When you have both finished, read each other's letters.

Now get out your calendars or appointment books, and make a date with each other to go to a place where you can get re-acquainted. You may decide to go out to dinner or go away for a weekend. Wherever you decide to go, your task is to begin to re-discover each other, to find out what is important to each of you at this stage in life. Ask each other questions about each other's dreams and aspirations. Discover new likes and dislikes. Above all, make each other feel welcome and honored.

After you have had your date, write letters to each other in your couple's journal. Write about a particular memory from your recent date. Tell each other how you felt being together and re-discovering each other. Then exchange the letters and read them.

The Conflict Stage

Romance frequently is interrupted by life. The honeymoon is over, or at least suspended for a time, while you butt heads with each other. Conflict is inevitable as you go about the incredibly complex job of managing your life together. While in the conflict stage of your relationship, the challenge is to work out your disagreements, power struggles, and differences so that you can draw close to each other once again.

The following exercise will give you practice in negotiating conflict. You may want to return to this exercise whenever you both feel you have reached an impasse in a particular issue in your relationship.

Exercise

Find a single, blank piece of paper, and put it on a table-top. Sit on opposite sides of this table. Imagine that the paper represents some value, goal, dream, or activity that is very, very important to each of you individually. Take a little time to think of what each of you wants the paper to represent. When you both have identified an important value, goal, dream, or activity, tell each other about it. Draw a line down the middle of the paper, and each write your value, goal, dream, or activity on your side of the paper.

When you are ready to begin the next part of this exercise, set a kitchen timer to ring in five minutes.

Without crumpling the paper, both grip it firmly. In this exercise, neither of you can commandeer the paper or simply take it away from the other. Both persons' hands must continue to hold onto the paper. If either of you tears the paper, neither of you gets what you wrote on it. During the five minutes, you must negotiate with each other who will get the paper and whatever is written there. After you have completed your negotiating, one of you must release the paper to the other. Remember to set the kitchen timer for five minutes before you begin.

After the five minutes are up, answer these questions individually in your couple's journal.

1. What feelings did you have as you told your partner what the paper represented for you?
2. How did you negotiate for the paper?
3. How did you feel about winning or losing the paper?
4. What was the outcome of your negotiating session?

Read each other's answers aloud.

The Commitment Stage

After negotiating and surviving conflict, maturing couples often enter the commitment stage. In the aftermath of conflict, renewed commitment to each other deepens your relationship. The conflict stage has shown you both that neither of you is completely wonderful or totally terrible. In the commitment stage you both have decided to accept each other, warts and all, and to tolerate each other's peculiarities, paradoxes, and puzzles. Renewed commitment to each other means your relationship as a couple will continue and you both will work to strengthen and deepen your life together.

The following exercise will help you use your couple's journal to verbalize your commitment to each other. This exercise is especially helpful after your relationship has weathered a significant conflict. Return to this exercise whenever you want to renew your commitment to each other.

Exercise

Take turns making a list in your couple's journal of your partner's five best and five worst qualities. List specific, concrete behaviors. For example:

Best	*Worst*
You are so gentle and well-mannered.	You are incredibly messy with your clothes.

After each of you makes a list of ten qualities, read your lists to each other.

Next write the following sentence under both lists:

I love you and I'm committed to the best and worst in you.

Then both sign your names underneath the sentence.
Close this exercise with a kiss.

The Creative Stage

Healthy couples not only work on their relationship together, they also work on their relationships with children, friends, church, and community. You have recovered health and happiness as a couple, and now you want to share that health and happiness with other significant relationships and the world in general.

This is the creative stage in your relationship. It is an inclusive stage—you both find you want to include other couples, families, friends, and even communities in your relationship. As a couple you find you have much in common with God's creation and you want your life together to have a positive, healthy impact on the world.

The following exercise is designed to help you move out into the world as a couple.

Exercise

Spend a week thinking separately about projects or activities you have always wanted to do together as a couple. Carry a piece of paper or small notebook around with you and, throughout the week, jot down any ideas you have. This week is a time for you to brainstorm. Any idea or dream is acceptable and must be recorded on your paper or in your little notebook. Let your imagination run wild! Be creative!

At the end of the week, re-read the lists you both have made. Each choose five ideas for projects or activities that are most important to you and number them one through five to indicate how important each idea is to the partner who thought of it. Assigning an idea the number one indicates that it is *very important*, a number five indicates that the idea is *least important*.

Schedule an appointment with your partner to discuss each other's list of five ideas.

When you meet together, share your lists of projects and activities. Negotiate and agree on two projects or activities you will undertake as a couple over the next six months. Record these two projects or activities in your couple's journal.

You have explored four stages in your life as a healthy couple. Remember that in the course of your life together you will return to each stage a number of times. Use the exercises in each stage to consciously work on your relationship.

Further Exercises for Your Couple's Journal

The following is a smorgasbord of other journaling exercises to complete as a couple. You may decide you want to experiment with all of these exercises, or you may decide that for now you'll do only one or two. Work on the exercises that are comfortable for you at this point in your relationship, choosing to work on exercises that are not only challenging but fun.

The Collage

This exercise is completely non-verbal. You cannot speak to each other while you are doing the exercise. It is designed to help you explore how you communicate without using words. In fact, you won't even write in your couple's journal until the end of the exercise. The collage exercise is a favorite with many couples who have tried it.

Exercise

Read through this entire exercise before you begin.

Together you will make a collage that is a picture of the current stage of your relationship. Remember the stages: romance, conflict, commitment, and creative.

Collect the following materials:

A sturdy piece of 8 1/2 X 11 construction paper or light cardboard.

Some paste or glue.

Two pair of scissors.
Several old magazines.

Clear a work space on a big table and put all the materials you've gathered on the table.

Discuss and decide what stage your relationship is in. Once you've agreed about the stage of your life together, you are not allowed to talk to each other again until the collage is finished.

Begin to look through the magazines, finding pictures that represent the feelings and experiences of this particular season of your life together. Cut out a picture and paste it on the construction paper or cardboard. Keep flipping through the magazines and clipping images that reflect how you feel during this stage of your life as a couple. Continue to work in this way until the paper is filled up or until you both run out of pictures to clip and paste.

During this part of the exercise, you may find you will have to negotiate for space on the paper or cardboard for the images you have clipped. Negotiate in silence! And no writing and passing notes to each other! Find other ways of communicating about how to make this collage together.

When you have finished the collage, both of you sign and date it. Then discuss these questions:

1. Describe the feelings you had as you worked on the collage.

2. Does the collage look like you worked separately? Or does it look as though your ideas and work are intertwined?

3. How difficult/easy was it for you to work together in silence?

4. What does your collage say about your stage of life as a couple right now? Does it look like an elaborate valentine, a battleground, or a work of modern art?

5. Did you enjoy making this collage?

Once you have thoroughly discussed your collage, tuck it between the pages of your couple's journal.

Return to this exercise any time you feel you need to explore a particular stage of your life together.

Fantasia

This is an active imagination exercise designed to bring your imaginative, unconscious lives into your relationship as a couple. Your individual unconscious is already having an impact on your relationship, and this exercise is a playful way to be aware of how your unconscious feels about your partner. Have fun with this exercise! Let your imaginations be free!

Exercise

You will take turns reading the exercise and imagining the exercise. Decide who will read first, while the other imagines.

The one who will do the active imagination exercise first must get into a comfortable, relaxing position—lie down on the couch, or sit in a comfortable chair with both feet on the floor.

The partner who reads the exercise must pause whenever there is a series of dots (. . . .). During the pause, the other partner should imagine the scene clearly, and then nod for the reading to continue.

When you are both ready, begin to read "Fantasia."

Fantasia

Close your eyes. You are in a strange place. You have never been here before. This place is called Fantasia. Is Fantasia an indoor or outdoor place? Look around you until you can see clearly. . . . Use all of your senses to explore Fantasia. See, hear, smell, feel, and perhaps even taste something to get acquainted with this new place. . . .

Now imagine I am with you in Fantasia. You can imagine me as myself, or you can imagine me in a symbolic way. I can be an animal, an object, a spirit, or another person such as royalty, a wizard or witch, a child. In Fantasia I can be anyone or anything you want me to be. Imagine me with you now in this new place. . . .

Now imagine yourself. In Fantasia you can be whoever or whatever you want to be. You can be an animal, an object, a spirit, or another person such as royalty, a wizard or witch, a child. Imagine yourself now in this new place. . . .

Now imagine us meeting together in Fantasia. When we meet, are we playful, serious, threatening, comfortable, or happy with each other? Imagine how it feels to meet me in Fantasia. . . .

We can say anything we want to each other. Or we can do something together. What do we say or do? Take your time imagining our encounter. . . .

Now it is time to say good-bye. We say good-bye. . . .

Fantasia melts from your mind.

Open your eyes.

Now trade places. The one who began the exercise by reading gets in a comfortable position to do the active imagination exercise. The other reads Fantasia aloud.

When you are finished, take turns writing in your couple's journal about Fantasia. Describe what Fantasia looked like for each of you. Describe your partner's appearance and behavior. Describe your own appearance and behavior. Describe your encounter with your partner in Fantasia. Finally, write about any feelings you had toward your partner in Fantasia.

Schedule a time with each other to read and discuss each other's experience in Fantasia.

Tell It Like It Is

Sometimes you may find that you each avoid saying things that might hurt your partner. In other words, you want to protect your partner's feelings, so you let a few things go unsaid. However, if much goes unspoken in your life as a couple, your relationship becomes one of "walking on eggs" around each other. It takes a lot of the fun out of a relationship when you are both too busy keeping silent and tiptoeing around each other's feelings.

This exercise helps you tell the truth in love to each other in a gentle, enjoyable way. It allows you both to be adults and take responsibility for your emotions and stop protecting each other. Neither of you is that fragile. Your couple's journal will be a safe place where you can tell each other how you really feel.

Exercise

Take turns completing the following sentences in your couple's journal:

When we are alone together, most of the time I'm . . .
When I tell you that I love you, it makes me feel . . .
When we are out together, I like to pretend . . .
If I told you what was really on my mind, I'm afraid you would . . .
I am attracted to you because . . .
More than with others, when I'm with you I refuse to feel . . .
What I'd like to get from you, but most often don't, is . . .
When I think of affirming you directly I begin to feel . . .
One thing I remember about us when I stroll down memory lane is . . .
Since I first met you, what I've learned about myself is . . .

When you've both finished the sentences, each read what the other has written. Take some time to discuss your feelings.

Create Your Own Exercises

Only your imaginations limit what you can do in your couple's journal. The exercises suggested here are just ideas to get you started on using your couple's journal to explore your life together. You may want to schedule some time together when you can create some exercises of your own. The only rule to making good exercises is to be creative and have fun!

Summary

In this chapter you have explored your life as a couple. You have experimented with a number of exercises that help you relate to each other in healthy, playful ways.

The quality of your life as a couple is the building block upon which your family is created and formed. The health of your family depends on the healthy relationship you cultivate as a couple. Return to this chapter often as you grow, change, and love each other through the stages of your life together.

8

Journaling About

Your Family

of Origin

Diaries record events of the day. Journals record events of the soul. We have seen that much of the work of recovery is in recovering our souls, observing and understanding the inner world of our emotions, dreams, and imaginations. Lasting recovery, however, requires that we understand our families of origin and how we still carry our original families inside us. In this chapter, you will discover how to get this inner family to work for your recovery—not against it.

You cannot escape the family of your childhood and youth. For better or worse, they are a part of you at this very moment. Parts of the father and mother of your youth continue to live inside you. Even the child you once were continues to live with you as your inner child. Each one of these family members has a daily impact on every one of your relationships. Your progress in recovery, in seeking healing for yourself and your relationships, is largely determined by how well you understand and work with your inner family. Your journal will be your most important tool in observing, understanding, and working with the family inside you.

Father

Each of us had a father. For good or ill, these men had a tremendous impact on how we grew up. Even if they were mostly absent during our childhood, the very absence shaped the persons we would become. Sometimes other fathering influences, like step-fathers or grandfathers, also had an impact on our young lives. But our actual fathers contributed significantly to how we came to understand who and what a father is.

That idea of who and what a father is continues with us as adults. We each have an internalized father—an inner image of father. In other words, we each have a father-self. We may not be very conscious of our father-selves, but they are there nonetheless, and they are very active in our lives and relationships. Our job in recovery is to get to know these father-selves and how they operate in our lives.

Some of us have inner father-selves who are fairly healthy. But many of us carry with us inner father-selves who are dysfunctional in some way. The particular condition of yours depends on three things: your experience of your actual, birth father; experiences you've had with other fathers in your life, as well as fathers you may have discovered in books; and, if you are a man, the adult experiences you have had in being a father to your children. If you are a woman, you will not be able to draw on an experience of being a father yourself, but you can still explore the experiences of your real father and your father-self.

The Positive Father

Take a few minutes to reflect on your birth father. Like my father, yours was probably a mixture of good and bad qualities as a parent. As you think about your father, begin by reflecting on his positive characteristics. When I think about my dad, I remember his integrity, warmth, and gentleness and his strong spirituality. As you remember the positive qualities in your father, think of a couple of examples from your childhood that show how these qualities were expressed. If, for example, gentleness was a characteristic of your father, think of a time when your father was gentle with you.

Once you have reflected on a couple of positive qualities in your father, complete the following journal exercise.

Exercise

The paragraph below is an active imagination exercise to help you further explore your father's positive characteristics. Find a box of crayons before you begin.

Close your eyes, and take a few long, deep, easy breaths. Let all of your muscles melt and relax. Read through the paragraph "Remembering Dad" before you begin to do the exercise.

Remembering Dad

Go back to your childhood. Summon a clear picture of your father's face. . . . Summon a memory of doing something fun with your dad. . . . Enjoy this experience of doing something fun with your dad as though you are doing it now. . . . Let your mind roam over other positive memories of Dad being with you or doing something with you. . . . Tell your father good-bye for now. . . .

Open your eyes and open your journal. Using your crayons with your non-dominant hand draw a picture of one of these positive memories with your father.

After you have finished your picture, record any thoughts or feelings that came to you as you drew this picture. Use your dominant hand and a pen to record your thoughts and feelings.

You have had a little exploration of your birth father. Now you are going to explore the internal father-self at work in your life today.

Like your real father, your father-self also has positive qualities. Your father-self is a blend of your experience of your real father combined with any other fathering influences you may have experienced in relationships, teachers, or books. For example, although I've never met the author C. S. Lewis, he has shaped positive qualities in my father-self.

The following is a list of several positive qualities you currently experience when your inner father-self is at work in your life and recovery.

- You manipulate your environment to your advantage. You are a "can do" person.
- You model integrity in difficult situations that require a moral solution.
- You maintain a sense of direction in your life and recovery. You know where you are going. You don't get overwhelmed by the details of existence.
- You use your fathering power non-abusively toward children by affirming them verbally and using warm, respectful touch.

- You model good judgment and spiritual discernment in the way you handle people and as you solve problems.
- You show children how to compete, cooperate, and collaborate using a wholesome mixture of love and limits.
- You ask forgiveness from yourself and others when you fail.

This exercise is designed to help you explore these positive qualities of your inner father-self.

Exercise

Read through this exercise before you begin it. Then close your eyes, and breathe deeply a few times. Let your muscles melt and relax.

Let your mind drift to a time when you experienced warm, competent fathering from a male relationship. For a moment remember and enjoy this warm, nurturing experience. . . .

Now let your mind form an image of your father-self. He may or may not look like your actual father. What does he look like? Get a clear picture of your father-self in your mind. . . .

Now open your eyes and open your journal. Write a dialogue with your father-self. Begin the dialogue by thanking your father-self for warm, nurturing fathering. Listen carefully to any reply from your father-self and record it in your journal.

Continue the dialogue between your conscious self and your father-self until you both have nothing more to say for now.

The Shadow Father

Your birth father was a mixture of good and bad qualities. He had a "shadow side," which is often characterized by two negative qualities: He was physically or emotionally absent from your youth, and/or he was excessive or addicted in some way.

I remember the shadow side of my father. I remember him being both physically and emotionally absent from my mother when she would fly into one of her rages. My mother would rage and scream and yell, but my father wouldn't address or confront her rage. Instead, he would mutter something about "a soft answer turneth away wrath" and quietly sneak through the back door to the church study. He made himself emotionally and physically absent when I needed him to deal with my out-of-control mother. When he went into that church study, he abandoned me to this raging woman.

Just as your real father had a shadow side, so does your father-self. Your father's negative qualities also shaped your inner father-self. And the shadow side of your father-self is also at work today in your adult life.

The shadow side of my own father contributed to the shadow side of my father-self. As a child, I learned that my father abandons me when he is faced with extreme emotions. Today, my father-self often fails to give me the courage I need to confront strong emotions in my life. When my real father went into that church study to get away from my mother, I went into my study, too. My study was in my head, where I could cut myself off from my own strong emotions. As an adult, my inner father-self continued to retreat into his study, my head, when faced with strong emotions in me or in those I love. That kind of behavior does not promote recovery. I needed to understand my father's and my father-self's shadow sides so that I could learn to handle strong emotions in healthy ways.

The following is a list of several negative qualities you experience when your father-self's shadow is active in undermining your life in general and your recovery in particular.

- You fail to take appropriate initiative. You do not praise others when praise is deserved; you do not confront when confrontation is needed.
- You have difficulty controlling anger or expressing anger appropriately.
- You fail to show curiosity. You become a mental and emotional "couch potato."
- You are not consistent raising your children. You flip-flop between permissiveness and harshness.
- You do not know how to make or keep friends.
- You do not consistently finish what you start. You have ideas, but they lack resolve or follow-through.
- Most importantly, you show an unwillingness or inability to bond

)ur children (this includes the inner children who also
p your family of self).

ving exercise is designed to help you identify part of your
hadow side and connect it with your continuing adult ex-

— Before you begin, you will need your box of cray-
— ons as well as your journal. Read through the exercise before starting.
— Close your eyes and summon the memory of
— a time when you saw the shadow side of your
father. Picture his face clearly. . . . Now picture his
behavior or actions that demonstrated his shadow side. Remember
the event clearly. . . . Remember the feelings you had toward your
father when you saw this shadow side of his personality. . . .

Staying with the feelings and the memory, open your eyes and
open your journal.

Using your box of crayons, with your non-dominant hand draw a
picture in your journal of the memory of your father's shadow side.
Put your feelings in this picture. Let it express how you felt on seeing
your father's shadow side.

After finishing your picture, write about your father's shadow and
the feelings you had remembering him in this way. Use a pen and
your dominant hand to record your experience. As John Bradshaw
says, "You can't heal what you can't feel,"[1] so write as honestly as
possible about your father and your feelings.

Now explore the shadow side of your father-self. Remember that
whatever shadow behavior you experienced in your real father also
shapes the development of your inner father-self. Therefore, your father-
self also has a shadow side to his personality, and it continues to have a
negative, unconscious impact on your recovery and relationships. It is
vital that you recognize the shadow in your father-self and consciously
understand how it impacts your adult life. The following exercise is designed to introduce the shadow side of your father-self to your conscious
mind.

Exercise

To complete this exercise you will need a large mirror, preferably full-length. Read this exercise before you begin.

Sit in a comfortable position and close your eyes. Take a few deep breaths and relax your muscles.

Once you are relaxed, let your imagination develop a picture of your shadow father-self. Develop a clear picture of your shadow father-self's facial expression. Is he angry, hurt, totally expressionless, sad, depressed? Take a few minutes to see your shadow father-self's facial expression in detail. . . .

Let your imagination give your shadow father-self a body. What does his posture convey to you—aggression, defeat, defiance? Does he slouch and shuffle along, or does he stomp and swing his fists? Get a clear picture of your shadow father-self's posture and movements. . . .

Keeping this image of your shadow father-self in front of you, open your eyes and stand in front of the mirror. Put your shadow father-self's facial expression on your face. Next, adapt your body to his posture. Imagine a typical sentence your shadow father-self might say, a sentence that summarizes his attitude and behavior. Examples of such sentences are: "I'm outta here, sweetheart"; "Leave me alone; I'm busy"; "Why can't you ever do anything right?"; or "I can't tell you how much that hurts me."

With your shadow father-self's facial expression on your face, your body conformed to his posture, and his attitude sentence on your lips, begin to walk back and forth in front of the mirror. Exaggerate his facial expression and posture. Repeat your shadow father-self's attitude sentence out loud. For a few minutes continue to walk back and forth in front of the mirror, exaggerating your movements, and repeating the sentence. Pay attention to what it feels like emotionally and physically to be your shadow father-self.

When you are finished, open your journal. Now that your conscious mind has met your shadow father-self, let him speak to you in your journal. Write as though you are still the shadow father-self you met in the mirror. Remember to use the first person, present tense (for example, "I'm tired and I don't have time for you").

When your shadow father-self has finished whatever he has to say, spend a few minutes responding to him. Tell him how you see him at work in your recovery and relationships. If necessary, challenge his behavior and perceptions. Close by telling him you are choosing to seek healing in your life and relationships.

God the Father

Finally, we are ready to explore God the Father and our relationship with him. God the Father originally made us in his image, and ever since we've returned the favor! All too often, our picture of God the Father is a confusing blend of the positive and shadow qualities of our human fathers. In other words, we make God into the image of our own fathers and father-selves. It is impossible to completely divorce our personal experience of fathers from that of God himself. But it is helpful to be aware of when we use our human fathers and father-selves to create our image of God.

The following exercise is designed to help you begin to sort out Father God from some of the other fathers in your life.

| **Exercise** | Open your journal. Write a letter to God the Father. Tell him that you know you have done a "make over" on him, making him into the image of your own external dad and your inner father-self. Tell God the Father how you see him now, and tell him how you feel when you are in his |

presence. For example, your letter might begin like this:

> *Dear Father,*
>
> *For too long I have had a secret picture in my mind of what you look like. You look too much like my grandfather with grey hair and a beard. But my grandfather wasn't around when I needed him as a kid. I need you, God, very much. I don't want you to be absent.*

Close the letter by telling God the Father how you see his good qualities developing inside you. Be sure to sign and date the letter.

The Child

Three different children live inside you. As you grew up, you were each of these children at different stages of your youth. During your infancy, you were still joined to your mother and father—you did not yet have a separate self. Your infant emotional life and that of your parents were one unit. At about age three, you began to develop a separate emotional life and identity. You were filled with curiosity, excitement, and wonder about the world around you. At ages three to six you were the child of wonder.

A few years later, you became a different child. You had responsibilities in school, you watched how your parents related to each other at home, and you learned something of what pain is like in life. The world had begun to weigh on you, and you became a child of sorrows.

Much later you entered adolescence. You were a mixture of energy, gleeful rebellion, anger, and other emotional moods. You played at living in an adult world while shedding your childhood. You became the child known as the "trickster."

The children hide in the adult and treat the adult the way the adult treats them. The face that you, the conscious adult, turn to your inner children is the same face they will turn to you. If you ignore them, they'll ignore you and you'll end up acting childish without knowing it. Whether you ignore them or acknowledge them, you and they are busy shaping one another and growing one another up or down.

In this section, you will explore your own inner child of wonder, child of sorrows, and the trickster. When you learn to take better care of these children, you learn to take better care of your self.

The Child of Wonder

That three-year-old child of wonder is still with you. This child has her nose pressed to the window pane as she goes down the freeway of life. William Blake describes this child as coming "fresh from heaven trailing streams of glory."[2] The child of wonder knows in his bones the miracle of his own life. He naturally commands attention and respect. He expects, without being showy, to receive adoration from anyone within hailing distance.

But the child's existence is delicate. It's like fresh, new spring grass with an ankle-high picket fence around it marked "Don't Walk on the Grass!" This child never grew up to be older than about three, and his existence remains fragile. When you begin to discover and experience the joy of your inner child of wonder, your shadow father-self will attempt to crush your child. The Bible gives us an example of the fragile nature of the child of wonder, and the shadow father's resolve to crush him or her. Just as the Christ child was being born in Bethlehem, King Herod was busy at the same time plotting to destroy him. Beware of your shadow father-self and experience the joy and spontaneity your child of wonder brings to your life.

Joseph, the Old Testament patriarch, let his own child of wonder shine through his life (see Genesis 37 and following). He had a bold sense of his own importance. He also possessed a solid sense of who he was in relation to God who sustained him amid the life-threatening trials of his young adulthood. A thirteenth century poet named Rumi captured the child of wonder in Joseph:

> Has anyone seen the boy who used to come here?
> Round-faced troublemaker,
> Quick to find a joke,
> Slow to be serious.
> Red shirt, perfect coordination, strong muscles—
> With things always in his pockets:
> A reed flute, an ivory pick.
> All ready for his immense talent.
> You know that one? Have you heard any stories of him?
> Pharaoh and the whole Egyptian world collapsed
> For want of such a Joseph.
> I'd gladly spend years getting word of him,
> Even third or fourth hand.[3]

The following exercise is designed to introduce you to your inner child of wonder. Return to this exercise whenever you feel stuck in your recovery or sense that your recovery is becoming boring or tedious. If you trust and care for your child of wonder, he or she will help you recover your sense of excitement, spontaneity, and discovery on your journey.

Exercise

Read this exercise before beginning.

Close your eyes and take a few deep, even breaths. Relax all of your muscles, and feel them melt away.

When you are fully relaxed, imagine your inner child of wonder. How old is this child? How is your child dressed? Where does your child of wonder live? Does anyone live with your child? Give yourself time to imagine your child of wonder completely. . . .

Carefully observe your inner child of wonder. What is he or she doing? . . . Now imagine yourself joining this child of wonder where he or she lives. . . . Feel yourself in the presence of this child of wonder. . . .

Keeping this scene fixed in your imagination, open your eyes and open your journal. Tell your child of wonder who you are—introduce yourself. Listen for a response from your inner child and record it in your journal. Your child of wonder may prefer to communicate with feelings rather than words. If so, record your child of wonder's emotional response to your presence with him or her. For example, you might write something like this:

I'm seeing your joy, now that I've joined you in this place.
Don't be afraid. I want to be your friend.

Continue to talk to your child of wonder and record the child's response until you feel it is time to go. When you feel it is time to leave, close your eyes again and hug your inner child goodbye. Then open your eyes and close your journal.

The Child of Sorrows

Like the child of wonder, the child of sorrows also continues to live inside you. Your inner child of sorrows is a few years older than your child of wonder. This child is old enough to experience and remember painful emotions.

Your child of sorrows absorbed the pain your family of origin never acknowledged or claimed. No emotion in a family is ever lost. Just because your family never spoke about feelings doesn't mean those feelings didn't exist. When a parent in your family of origin felt an emotion, but didn't claim or acknowledge it, the children made that emotion their own.

For example, if the father is frequently angry, but takes no responsibility for his anger, a child usually claims the father's anger. The child will say to himself, "I must have made Daddy angry. If I were different, or a better boy, Daddy wouldn't get so mad."

The child who most frequently picks up unclaimed emotional articles at the family lost and found is the child of sorrows. Your inner child of sorrows is old enough to experience powerful negative emotions and to absorb them like a sponge. This child has been collecting family members' powerful negative emotions for years. Your child of sorrows is your wounded inner child.

At some point on your recovery journey, you must recover your wounded inner child of sorrows. Listening, loving, and caring for your child of sorrows brings deep, lasting healing. The following exercise is designed to introduce you to your child of sorrows. Return to this exercise whenever you feel ashamed of yourself, but can't figure why. Your child of sorrows can tell you what is going on. This exercise is also useful when you are feeling depressed, but can find no immediate reason for it. Your child of sorrows may be able to help.

Exercise

Read this exercise before beginning.

Close your eyes, take deep breaths, and relax all of your muscles.

When you are completely relaxed, imagine your child of sorrows. What does this child look like? How old is your child of sorrows? How is this child dressed? Where does your child of sorrows live? What does this place look like? Take a few moments to completely imagine your child of sorrows. . . .

Focus on what your child of sorrows is doing. . . . Imagine yourself standing by this inner child in his or her world. . . . Feel what it is like to be with this child. . . .

Sometimes you must be prepared to learn that this little child-self has been so severely wounded that he or she is dead or almost dead. But you must also realize that what is dead within the psyche does not have to remain dead. God has the power today to raise these part-selves from the dead, just as he has in days gone by. You must sometimes stand beside God before the tomb and gently attend it quietly until the time is right, when God will say, "Child, come forth!"

In moments like that, when "the hearts of the fathers are turned toward the children" (Mal. 4:6), the dead, shamed child-selves within us whose hearts have been broken return to the land of the living. When this happens within me or within another, my heart is hushed and awed.

Keeping this world of your child of sorrows before your mind's eye, open your eyes and your journal. Introduce yourself to your wounded inner child. Listen for this child's response and record it in your journal. Let yourself feel whatever emotions may be coming from your child of sorrows, and record these feelings in your journal.

You also may find your child of sorrows is angry or suspicious. You may have to do this exercise several times before your wounded inner child comes to trust you with his or her feelings.

I remember how difficult this exercise was for me at first. My child of sorrows was about eight years old. His heart was heavy from loneliness and rage. He had been collecting these powerful, unclaimed feelings from his family for years and years. When I found him, he was standing in the side yard of our old house throwing a pocket knife at the side of a tree. He was pretending to be Davy Crockett. I interrupted his game and recorded our conversation in my journal:

WHO ARE YOU?

i'm the grown-up you became. i'm coming to visit you to let you know i survived. i feel bad you are alone and bored.

I'M OKAY. YOU CAN GO NOW. I DON'T NEED YOUR PITY. SEE YA.

so, you're mad at me.

YOU'RE NOT TOO TOUGH. YOU DON'T STAY FOR LONG. THEN YOU SPLIT. I'M SICK OF IT.

sorry. wanna play catch? i can stay for a while. i'll do better down the line. i promise.

WELL OKAY. I SUPPOSE YOU'RE BETTER THAN NOBODY. I'LL GET MY BALL AND GLOVE. I WANT TO PRACTICE PITCHING HARD AT YOU.

okay, long as i get to wear the glove.

When you feel your conversation is over, close your eyes and say goodbye to each other. If you like, promise to come back soon to visit your wounded child.

The Trickster

The jubilation of the child of wonder and the pain of the child of sorrows are mixed together in the trickster, who lives on inside you from your late childhood and adolescence. This inner child is still rebelling against misused authority in your dysfunctional family of origin. He automatically knows who *not* to respect and shows his disrespect by shooting bullets of anger into any authority figure he encounters. But his favorite shooting target is you. Your grown-up self is the ultimate authority figure at whom your trickster aims his anger. Your inner trickster is full of energy, mischief, and rebellion.

Jacob, the patriarch in Genesis 25, is a biblical example of a man whose inner trickster was always at work. Jacob deceived his father and tricked his brother, Esau, out of his birthright. He became involved in an elaborate, lengthy plot to win the woman of his dreams, only to be tricked by his father-in-law. Jacob's life was filled with plots and counterplots to subvert authority.

The following exercise is designed to introduce you to your inner trickster. Return to this exercise whenever you think you may be engaging in self-defeating behavior. It is just possible your inner adolescent child is up to his or her old tricks again. The goal is to get to know your trickster and persuade this child to become a friend instead of always being a teen-aged enemy.

Exercise

Read this exercise before you begin.

You will need a mirror, preferably full-length, to complete this exercise.

Close your eyes, breathe deeply, and relax all your muscles.

Imagine your inner trickster. Summon that part of you who is street-smart, savvy, manipulative; the one who wants to do unto others before they do unto him or her. Feel the part of you who uses cunning, power, and even helplessness to defeat your best adult efforts. Spend some time focusing on what this trickster looks like. Imagine his or her facial expression and the attitude his or her posture communicates. . . .

Once you have a clear picture of the trickster in mind, open your eyes and go to the mirror. Put on your inner trickster's facial expression. Adopt the trickster's posture in your body. Exaggerate the trickster's facial expression and posture in your body. Create a sentence that fits your trickster's attitude. Such a sentence might be: "I'll be there for you—honest!"; "I promise I'll never do that again"; "Hey, who needs you?"; "I'm lookin' out for Number One!"; or "Don't tell *me* what to do!"

Now walk back and forth in front of the mirror, repeating your trickster's attitude sentence aloud. Get a good feeling for how your inner trickster looks, acts, and talks. How does it feel to be a trickster?

After you've been the trickster for a little while, open your journal and label the top of a fresh page: "My Trickster." Write in your journal as though you are your inner trickster. Start by boasting a little. Make yourself a little larger than life. Let your trickster display his or her power.

Then become your conscious, adult self. Make friends with your trickster. Tell him or her how much you appreciate his or her savvy and smarts. Be sure to say that you understand how much the tricks were necessary for you to survive your earlier life. Offer to be friends with your trickster.

Listen for any response your trickster may make and record it in your journal. Continue the dialogue for as long as you like.

When you are finished, say goodbye to each other for now.

The Mother

Your mother-self is a patchwork quilt of your actual birth mother and other mothers you have experienced and read about. Like your father-self, your mother-self is a mixture of positive and negative qualities. There are at least three parts to your mother-self. One part is the tender life-giver, the one who gives birth. The second part is responsible for the growth and health of the child. And the third part takes away life, corrupts growth, and limits development. In Greek mythology, the three Fates are feminine. One pulls the thread of each person's life out of a long spool; one measures the length of life to be given each person; and one snips the thread. Kali, a goddess of India, is usually depicted as a two-faced woman whose different sides share a common backbone. One side tenderly breast-feeds a child while the other eats the child's guts. These symbols demonstrate the different faces of the mother and the mother-self.

Your mother-self continues to live inside you long after you have left home. She is a powerful influence on your recovery and relationships. Your mother-self can either bring new growth or attempt to defeat the process of healing and wholeness. Therefore, it is crucial that you meet your mother-self and understand how she continues to operate in your life.

The following exercise will help you reflect on various mothering influences. These mothering influences contribute to the construction of your inner mother-self. If you are a man, exercises that examine your mother-self may prove difficult, but don't give up. With patience and work you can get in touch with your inner mother.

Exercise

Open your journal and label a fresh page: "My Mother-self."

Take a few minutes to list all of the women who have had a mother-like influence on your life. This list will probably include your birth mother. Your list may also include other female relatives, such as aunts and grandmothers. Secular and Sunday school teachers may be on your list. Don't forget to include any mothers you have read about in books. Include on this list women who have had negative mothering influences on your life. For example, some people experience an older sister as a negative mothering influence; this sister is someone who was always telling you what to do and how to behave.

When you have completed your list, re-read it. Then make a list of the characteristics each of these women contributed toward creating your inner mother-self. You will probably list negative as well as positive characteristics. This list could include:

- Love, compassion
- Humor, fun
- Constricting, lots of rules and regulations
- Faithful, godly
- Too absent, not often at home for me
- Challenging me to adventure
- Soft and demure
- Tough and inflexible

Your list will be a mixture of characteristics that are conflicting. That's okay. Your mother-self is a complex, powerful blend of positive and negative qualities. Identifying those qualities is the first step to understanding this part of yourself.

When you have finished making your lists, close your journal for now.

The Positive Mother

Your mother-self has a lot to offer you on your recovery journey. This is a list of positive qualities you experience when your inner mother-self is active in your life and recovery.

- You live in your own body well. You know your body's needs, rhythms, and limits.
- You are able to empathize with other people's feelings in an appropriate, healthy way.
- You are able to establish and maintain emotionally intimate relationships.

- You are wise. You apply factual knowledge to the ordinary events in life.
- You intuitively understand the need for your own physical and emotional comfort. You know how to be comfortable in your environment. You share this comfort with others.
- You know and enjoy the beauty inside yourself, in others, and in the world.
- You are very practical and pragmatic about life and faith.
- You enjoy your recovery journey. In fact, you are more interested in the journey than the destination.
- You value cooperation over competition. You enjoy making connections with people more than being separated from them.

Since your mother-self was significantly shaped by your birth mother, you need to explore her positive qualities. The following exercise is designed to help you remember some of the good times with your mom.

Exercise

Read this exercise before you begin.

Close your eyes, breathe deeply, and relax your muscles.

Let your mind drift back to your childhood. Skim your memory, and select a few memories of your mother when you were a child. Perhaps you remember laughing together; licking batter from the bowl when Mom baked a cake; Mom reading bedtime stories to you; or how your mom rescued you from the neighborhood bully.

When you have a few memories of these good times in mind, open your eyes and open your journal. Briefly describe each memory. After each memory, write a positive mothering characteristic the memory taught you. For example, you might record a memory and positive mothering characteristic that looks like this:

Memory: I remember Mom tucking me into bed on a stormy night. First she got me all snuggled in bed. Then she took my hand and said a prayer for sweet dreams and protection from the scary sounds the storm made. I felt warm and safe with her bending over me.

Characteristic: I learned what nurturing feels like from this memory. Part of nurturing is making me, or someone I love, feel warm and safe.

When you have finished recording your memories and positive mothering characteristics, read them aloud to yourself. Close this exercise by thanking God for these gifts from your mom.

Now you are ready to further explore the inner mother-self you have developed over the years. Your mother, your mother-self has many positive qualities. The following exercise will help you experience those positive mothering qualities you carry around inside you. They are the roots of self-care and self-nurturing necessary to any recovery journey. Once you identify these qualities, they will be available to you at any time for comfort and care.

Exercise

Read this exercise before beginning.

Close your eyes, breathe deeply, and relax all of your muscles.

Imagine your mother-self. Get a clear picture of her in your mind's eye. What does she look like? Is she young, old, or ageless in appearance? How is she dressed? What do her surroundings look like? Is your mother-self alone, or does she appear with others? . . .

Feel your mother-self radiate goodness throughout your body. . . .

When you have a clear picture of your mother-self and you sense her goodness, open your eyes and open your journal. Write in your journal how you feel about your mother-self at this moment in time. If you have questions for her, ask them in your journal. Then pause in your writing and listen for a response from her. Record her response in your journal. Continue to write a dialogue with your mother-self until you feel there is nothing left to say.

Close this exercise by closing your eyes and saying goodbye to her for now.

The Shadow Mother

Just as there was a shadow side to your father's personality, your mother had a dark, shadowy aspect as well. Most likely, your relationship with your mother was not perfect. She was a flawed individual, and those flaws affected her relationship with you.

The following exercise is designed to bring your mother's shadow side to the forefront of your memory. Remember, the negative qualities you experienced from your mother shaped the mother-self you carry with you daily.

This exercise is not easy to do. It is hard to remember our fathers' shadow sides; but it is often harder to look at our mothers' shadows. So take it easy on yourself. If this exercise is too painful, stop and continue it later when you feel ready. Understanding the shadow side of your mother will help you later in identifying the shadow of your mother-self, who has a significant impact on your progress in recovery.

Exercise

Simply let your mind drift back to memories of your mother from your childhood. Remember the shadows in your relationship with her. These memories may include the times she left you alone or frightened you; times she teased you in front of your friends; times when she may have punished you excessively; or times she seemed jealous of your looks or talents. Select a few of these memories to record in your journal.

Open your journal. Briefly record each memory of seeing your mother's shadow side. After each memory, record a negative mothering quality you learned from that memory. For example, your journal might look like this:

Memory: I remember when Mom left me in kindergarten on my first day in school. I was terrified and tried to cling to her. But she just pried my hands from her arms and walked away.

Characteristic: Sometimes Mom chose to not be there for me or to abandon me. I sometimes practice this negative mothering quality. I abandon myself every time I don't take care of my emotional needs.

When you have finished recording your memories and their negative mothering characteristics, close your eyes and imagine Jesus holding you close to him. Be with Jesus for as long as you like. Then open your eyes and close your journal.

It is important to identify negative qualities in your real mother because those negative qualities live on inside in your shadow mother-self. When your shadow mother-self is active in your life, you experience her in a number of ways. The following is a list of several negative mothering qualities you may experience when your shadow mother-self is at work in your life:

- You lose touch with your body. Of course, you are still inside your body, but you feel like a foreigner living in a strange land.
- You lose balance in your relationships and become an isolate or merger artist. The *isolate* cuts himself off not only from others, but from the self as well. His feelings are cut from his thinking, restraint is separated from his impulses, and any sense of being is totally absent from his doing. This merger artist loses all boundaries: "I am you; you are me; we are we."
- You are prone to addiction. You become an addiction looking for a place to happen. The addiction can be alcohol or another substance, sex, work, thrills and spills, or a variety of people and/or activities. The addiction of choice is *more*!
- You are earth-bound and you lose the forest because of all the trees. You get so occupied with minutia that matters of vision and spirit are lost. You work hard organizing teams to clear the swamp, but you don't see that you are trying to clear the wrong swamp.
- You are unbounded with impulses and relationships, unable to contain yourself. Under pressure, your emotions squirt over those around you like a viscous mist. You might wear a button saying, "I tried to contain myself, but I escaped!"
- You suck on others, stealing their emotional supplies, as though you'd stuck a big straw in another's chest and begun sucking. Gradually the liveliness gets drained out of those around you and you begin to feel better.
- You are victim to enfeeblement and death by poisoning. Your thoughts and feelings are tainted with unwarranted negativism.

You are caught in the grip of a perverse moodiness toward yourself and others.

This exercise is designed to help you identify your shadow mother-self. This exercise is rewarding, but difficult. The goal is to get to know your shadow mother-self, identify these negative mothering qualities at work in your life, and transform negative qualities into positive, nurturing ones. You may need to return to this exercise several times before you begin to experience positive transformation.

Exercise

Read this exercise before beginning. You will need a full-length mirror.

Close your eyes and imagine your shadow mother-self. Picture her face and posture as clearly as you can. Imagine her age, appearance, and clothing. . . .

For a few moments, focus on her face. What kind of facial expression does she have? Then look at her posture, the way she holds her body. Get a clear picture of her body in your mind's eye. . . .

Open your eyes and go to the mirror. Put your shadow mother-self's facial expression on your face. Adopt her posture in your body. Look at your shadow mother-self in the mirror. . . .

Create a sentence that summarizes your shadow mother-self's attitude toward you. Such a sentence might be: "I love to eat little children like you"; "You'll never amount to anything"; or "I gave you the best years of my life and all you do is disappoint me."

Walk back and forth in front of the mirror repeating your shadow mother-self's attitude sentence aloud. Feel what it is like to be this woman. . . .

After you have spent a few minutes being your shadow mother-self, open your journal. Write a couple of paragraphs in your journal telling your shadow mother-self what it feels like to be in her presence. Tell her how in the future you will recognize the way she is operating in your life. Tell her you are sick and tired of her hiding in nooks and crannies, waiting to ruin your recovery. Listen for her response and record her answers in your journal.

Choose a positive mother-self quality that offers you nurture and comfort. Spend a few minutes writing about how this positive mothering quality counteracts the negative influences of your shadow mother-self. Then close your journal.

Confronting your shadow mother-self may prove to be difficult. But she is always there inside you, seeking to undermine your recovery. When you are able to identify how your shadow mother-self is at work in your life, you can call on your positive mother-self for nurture, care, and healing. And those negative mothering qualities will be transformed into experiences of growth and recovery.

Summary

In this chapter you've learned to journal with your inner family. You have identified those negative qualities that thwart recovery, and you have learned to identify those positive qualities in your inner father, children, and mother that promote healing and growth.

Take care of your inner family of self. Use your journal to speak with each member of this family often. Your inner father, mother, and children will give you priceless information about how your recovery is working in all of your significant relationships. When you take care of your inner family, even the shadowy members of the family, they will take care of you.

A
Final
Word

Your journals record your life as you search for healing and wholeness for yourself and your relationships. We hope that the material and exercises in this book have deepened and enriched your recovery. We also hope you enjoyed beginning your journal. Remember, as you continue on your journey, that your journal will show you are a recovering believer who leaves visible tracks in the sand.

Notes

Chapter 1

1. Thich Nhat Hanh, *Being Peace* (Berkeley: Parallax Press, 1987). Used by permission.

2. Matt. 13:34.

Chapter 2

1. John Bradshaw, *Healing the Shame That Binds You* (Deerfield Beach: Health Communications, 1988).

Chapter 3

1. Edward Hoffman, *The Right to Be Human: A Biography of Abraham Maslow* (Los Angeles: Jeremy Tarcher, 1988) in David Feinstein and Peg Mayo, *Rituals for Living and Dying* (San Francisco: Harper, 1990).

2. Virginia Stem Owens, *And the Trees Clap Their Hands* (Grand Rapids: Eerdmans, 1983).

Chapter 4

1. G. B. Harrison, ed., *Selected Poems of Rainer Maria Rilke* (New York: Harper & Row, 1981).

Chapter 5

1. Robert Bly, ed., *Selected Poems of Rainer Maria Rilke* (New York: Harper & Row, 1981).

2. Marcel Proust, *Remembrance of Things Past* (New York: Random House, 1982) in David Feinstein and Peg Mayo, *Rituals for Living and Dying* (San Francisco: Harper, 1990), 40.

3. John 8:32.

4. C. S. Lewis, *The Narnia Chronicles* (New York: Collier, 1953).

Chapter 6

1. C. S. Lewis, *The Narnia Chronicles.*

Chapter 8

1. John Bradshaw, *Healing the Shame That Binds You.*

2. William Blake, as told by Michael Mead in a workshop sponsored by the Lost Dog Men's Council, Santa Monica, CA, September, 21–22, 1990.

3. A. J. Arberry, ed., *Mystical Poems of Rumi, Persian Heritage Series No. 23* (Boulder: Westview, 1979).

Bibliography

Bankson, Marjory Z. *Seasons of Friendship: Naomi and Ruth As a Pattern*. San Diego: LuraMedia, 1987.

Benson, Bod, and Michael W. Benson. *Disciplines for the Inner Life*. Waco: Word, 1985.

Bly, Robert. *Iron John: A Book About Men*. New York: Addison-Wesley, 1990.

Bradshaw, John. *Healing the Shame That Binds You*. Deerfield Beach: Health Communications, 1989.

———. *Homecoming*. New York: Bantam, 1990.

Buscaglia, Leo. *The Fall of Freddie the Leaf*. New York: Holt, Rinehart and Winston, 1982.

Campbell, Susan. *The Couple's Journey: Intimacy As a Path to Wholeness*. San Luis Obispo: Impact, 1980.

Capacchione, Lucia. *The Creative Journal: The Art of Finding Yourself*. North Hollywood: Newcastle, 1989.

Covey, Stephen R. *The Seven Habits of Highly Effective People*. New York: Summit, 1990.

Feinstein, David, and Stanley Krippner. *Personal Mythology: The Psychology of Your Evolving Self*. Los Angeles: Jeremy Tarcher, 1988.

BIBLIOGRAPHY

Hall, Calvin. *The Meaning of Dreams*. New York: McGraw-Hill, 1966.

Johnson, Robert. *She: Understanding Feminine Psychology*. New York: Harper & Row, 1977.

————. *Inner Work: Using Dreams and Active Imagination for Personal Growth*. New York: Harper & Row, 1986.

Kelsey, Morton. *Dreams: A Way to Listen to God*. New York: Paulist, 1978.

Lloyd, Roseanne, and Richard Solly. *Journey Notes: Writing for Recovery and Spiritual Growth*. Minneapolis: Hazeldon, 1989.

Mason, Mike. *The Mystery of Marriage*. Portland: Multnomah, 1985.

Miller, Stuart. *Men and Friendship*. Boston: Houghton Mifflin, 1983.

Millett, Craig B. *In God's Image: Archetypes of Women in Scripture*. San Diego: LuraMedia, 1990.

Moore, Robert, and Douglas Gillette. *King, Warrior, Magician, and Lover*. San Francisco: HarperCollins, 1990.

————. *The King Within*. San Francisco: HarperCollins, 1992.

Progoff, Ira. *At a Journal Workshop*. New York: Dialogue House, 1975.

Rupp, Joyce. *The Star in My Heart: Experiencing Sophia, Inner Wisdom*. San Diego: LuraMedia, 1990.

Sanford, John. *Dreams: God's Forgotten Language*. New York: Lippincott, 1968.

Smalley, Gary, and John Trent. *The Blessing*. Nashville: Thomas Nelson, 1986.

William, Stephron. *The Jungian-Senoi Dreamwork Manual*. Berkeley: Journey Press, 1985.

About the Authors

Drs. Vance Lee and Bethyl Joy Shepperson, licensed psychologists, direct Shepperson Psychological Associates, a Christian-based private practice group in Fullerton, California, offering individual, couple, and group counseling.

Bethyl holds the Psy.D. in Clinical Psychology from Rosemead School of Psychology of Biola University. She works primarily with women recovering from incest, molestation, and physical and sexual abuse. She supervises group leaders and acts as consultant to VIRTUES (Victims of Incest: Recovery through Understanding, Education, and Support), in Orange County, California.

Vance holds the Ph.D. in Clinical and Community Psychology from the University of South Florida. He specializes in working with men and their recovery issues.

For information concerning treatment programs, please contact:

Dr. Vance Shepperson or Dr. Bethyl Shepperson
Shepperson Psychological Associates, Inc.
680 Landorff Drive, Suite 217
Fullerton, California 92631